BUSINESS BEHAVIOR, VALUE AND GROWTH

Revised Edition

BUSINESS BEHAVIOR, VALUE AND GROWTH

Revised Edition

WILLIAM J. BAUMOL

PRINCETON UNIVERSITY

Harcourt, Brace & World, Inc.

New York / Chicago / San Francisco / Atlanta

The first edition of this book was published
by The Macmillan Company, New York, 1959.

Library of Congress Catalog Card Number: 67–14320

Printed in the United States of America

TO HILDA

Preface to the revised edition

Happily, during the two-year period when this book was out of print, I received many complaints about its unavailability. I therefore found it easy to convince myself of the desirability of a new edition. The changes in this revised edition are easily described. The two most substantial changes are the inclusion with some modifications of my growth equilibrium model of the firm (Chapter 10) and of a new model designed to investigate the long-run effects of increased growth on effective demand (Chapter 11). I have also made some corrections in the appendix to Chapter 3, eliminated some of my more naïve propositions on corporation finance, and added a few comments on the literature that has appeared since the publication of the first edition (Chapter 6). Two chapters that seemed on rereading to say very little were dropped. These, together with a little expository emendation here and there and the insertion of a few references that should have been included earlier, constitute the sum and substance of the modifications introduced into the new edition.

Though the very reappearance of the book indicates that there has been no basic change in my position, I should like to affirm this explicitly. Of course, on some details my views on the subject have changed, but in general I remain unreconstructed. I do not believe that all firms need have the same objectives, and I think I have succeeded in demonstrating that objectives other than profit maximization are also amenable to rigorous analysis. Whether we accept sales or growth maximization as reasonable approximations to the objectives of most firms today, is not, to me, the central issue. Rather, I will have made my basic point if the profession comes to accept the views that the goals of the firm cannot be determined by a priori considerations, even on the assumption of entrepreneurial rationality, and that the consequences of other company targets can usefully be subjected to theoretical investigation.

In addition to the debts acknowledged in the preface to the first edition I must thank Philip Howrey, Burton Malkiel, R. E. Park, Harold Shapiro, and John Williamson for their extremely valuable comments, which saved me from a number of errors and enabled me to improve the exposition at several points. I must also express my gratitude to the National Science Foundation and to the Ford Foundation, whose grants greatly facilitated the work of revision.

WILLIAM J. BAUMOL

Princeton, New Jersey
April 1966

Preface to the first edition

The book makes no pretense at being a treatise. No attempt has been made to offer a well-rounded discussion of any of its subjects. The reader will doubtless note many serious omissions and cases wherein important elements are inadequately stressed. These he will have to supply for himself or apply from elsewhere in the literature. In almost every case I included items only where I felt I had something, however minor, to contribute in novelty of analysis or exposition. I hope it is not too much of an abuse of the reader to ask him to put up with the unbalanced treatments that result.

The book is made up of two only slightly related parts: the first is a study of static oligopoly theory; and the second contains materials on the theory of economic development—some of which build on results from Part I. The result of this variegated subject matter is that, while I would hope most of the volume is of some interest to the theorist, I can hardly expect all of it to hold the attention of those who are mainly concerned with the formulation of policy for economic development. To any such readers, in addition to Part II, I can conscientiously recommend only Chapter 6 and possibly Chapters 5, 7, and 8 of Part I.

The order in which the various parts of the book were written may be of some interest because the methodological discussion of Chapter 1 may easily appear to be a hastily cooked up rationalization for the rather unrigorous theorizing of Part II and the casual empiricism of the entire volume. I must point out that this chapter was completed long before the rest of the book and that parts of it appeared in print as early as 1953. Most of Part I of the book was written well after the rest of the manuscript—about two months before it was sent off to the publisher. This is largely the result of my own stubborn reluctance to part company with the universal applicability of the profit maximization hypothesis. Only after a number of unsuccessful attempts to force its implications down the throats of otherwise highly cooperative firms for which I was consulting did it occur to me that something might be wrong with the central tenets of my position. After that I still tried to defend its remaining outposts as, one after another, they seemed to fall before the onslaught of the facts. Just quite recently the entire structure of my position became clear to me, and even then, most of the theorems in Chapter 7 and applications in Chapter 8 took me by surprise as they emerged from the mathematics or discussions of various specific problems.

One comment on Part II is also worth making. In discussing development I have not given much attention to unemployment and its related problems. Of course I believe that depressions can retard growth and that we should do everything possible to combat them, including use of the powerful techniques that Keynes brought to our attention. I have not repeated this in the book for two reasons: first, because I have nothing to add to the standard literature on this matter; and, second, because I wish to emphasize, by overstatement, if necessary, that an effective program for accelerated economic growth requires more than a reproclamation of unrelenting war with the depression of the 1930's.

If the manuscript still lacks theoretical rigor or practical good judgment it is not for lack of the good offices of the many friends who have read the manuscript at various stages, contributed a number of its basic ideas, and dissuaded me from what now appear to me to have been my worst follies. Most helpful of all have been Professors Harvey Leibenstein and George Stolnitz. The crucial contributions of the former and the painstakingly detailed suggestions of the latter have been invaluable to me. In addition I owe profound gratitude to Wroe Alderson, Lester Chandler, Robert Dorfman, F. L. Fletcher, T. W. Hutchison, Gardner Patterson, Ralph Turvey, and Jacob Viner. The London School of Economics contributed once again to my writing by providing an atmosphere of remarkable intellectual ferment and kind hospitality during the last few months of work on the manuscript. Last, and I need hardly add, not least, thanks are due to the Guggenheim Foundation and Princeton University, whose generous grants permitted the completion of the book.

I acknowledge the kindness of the editors of *Economica*, *Kyklos*, and *The Review of Economics and Statistics* in giving their permission to reproduce materials that first appeared in these publications. The book also contains excerpts from a piece that was originally published in a compendium of papers submitted to the Joint Economic Committee of The Congress of the United States.

WILLIAM J. BAUMOL

Princeton, New Jersey
May 1959

Contents

Chapter 5. Funds limitations and profits

Chapter 6. The revenue maximization hypothesis

Chapter 7. A static oligopoly model

Chapter 8. Some implications of the oligopoly model

PART II
ON THE THEORY OF ECONOMIC GROWTH

Chapter 9. Introduction to Part II

Chapter 10. Growth in the activity of the firm

BUSINESS BEHAVIOR, VALUE AND GROWTH

Revised Edition

CHAPTER 1

Methodology

In writing this volume I intended to employ questionable premises and to use them to obtain questionable conclusions.[1] This may seem a goal of doubtful merit, but it is superior to its alternative—the building of irrefutable theorems into an empty edifice of compounded tautologies.

This prescription is really not easy to follow, though I fear subsequent parts of this volume will make it seem all too effortless—for it is usually tempting to take refuge in the more or less indisputable by pruning away all statements that are likely to conflict with "reality." Of course, many of us have employed monstrous constructions that we have tried to convince ourselves are good approximations to the economy in which we live, but it is not my desire to emulate this practice, which indeed may be the worst of all possible worlds.

1. The functions of an economic model

What can we hope for from our theoretical models? They necessarily involve oversimplifications and abstractions, but with their aid we get as close as we can to what the natural scientist does in setting up a model on which to base an experiment to be conducted under artificial laboratory conditions; thus, the elements omitted from our model correspond to the variables that are held constant in a controlled experiment. A useful model describes an imaginary world sufficiently complex and similar to reality to permit us to make some legitimate inferences about the behavior of the economy but at the same time sufficiently simple for us to understand and manipulate with the tools at our disposal. The facts of the problem on hand and the questions being asked must decide what we can afford to leave out and what we must put in to avoid being misled. Thus, a model can only be designed around and

[1]The word "questionable" refers to an assertion that may be plausible but can only be verified by empirical investigation. In other words, a questionable assertion is one that can be questioned by the facts (and hence cannot be a tautology).

judged in light of a specific problem. By "a problem" I do not necessarily mean a question of public policy; I refer, rather, to any well-defined question involving an exploration of economic relationships of the form: "What will be the effect on y of such and such a change in x_1 or x_2 when the behavior of the other relevant variables, $x_3, \ldots, x_n$ is such and such?"

Such a model can never have general validity. Only the classification and tautology toward which economic theorists lean in their more timid moments can have this property, and from them we can learn relatively little. To find useful approximations, we must work with half-truths. This is because reality is too complex for our weak analytic ability, because our data are incomplete, and because observation, no matter how complete, can only discover correlations, not the structural relationships we seek for our theory. Facts, unfortunately, never speak for themselves, and we must be prepared to choose among the many alternative hypotheses that can be found to account for any set of observed relationships.

Because our models are only half-truths, in new applications we may have to start afresh, retailoring our premises to approximate the changed facts of the case. We must recognize that a model that sheds some light on one situation can be worse than useless and totally misleading in another—because elements which can in one case be dismissed as unimportant and left out of the construction may in another situation be crucial. We must reexamine our assumptions for relevance in every case where we seek to apply a theoretical analysis; and, where our model seems to provide some guidance, we must constantly be on the lookout lest its oversimplification mislead us into facile conclusions and mistaken policy measures.

This position may seem innocuous enough, but it is in direct conflict with other methodological points of view, several of which are rather widely held.

2. Alternative methodological positions: generalization

There is the view that greater generality in theoretical results is inherently desirable. Sometimes it is almost suggested that the theorist's ultimate aim should be to obtain results of universal validity. Of course it must be admitted that results that are applicable everywhere would be highly desirable if they could be obtained without paying too high a price; but it is my feeling that generalization is very costly and that these costs are often *not* given adequate attention. A theoretical construct which seeks to be applicable to a variety of circumstances must abstract from the peculiar characteristics of each situation, and that construct is, therefore, useful only when we are interested in whatever properties they happen to have in common.

In most situations there are likely to be present some particular relationships that *do* concern us and that, because they are not omnipresent, limit the generality of our model. Reality presents us with problems and situations that are structurally very different. The extreme case, the perfectly general model, must abstract from everything or, what is very close to the same thing, take account of everything and so degenerate into a taxonomy.

In my view a useful model will usually be appropriate only in particular circumstances and, even then, only for the analysis of particular problems. Clearly, where greater generality can be achieved without loss of content, we must approve of it—but this is rarely possible. It is my plea that we follow our own good advice as economists and balance off costs against advantages in deciding on the level of generality at which we wish to operate our research.[2]

Sometimes the issue is confused by calling a model generally valid if it is appropriate every time the circumstances and problems to which it is relevant are repeated precisely.[3] A determinist is forced to insist that in this sense every *valid* model is perfectly *general* and that in fact the two terms are synonymous. I do not want to quarrel with word usage, and I only point out that it is not generalization in this sense that is questioned here; rather, my difference is with those writers who have substituted classification for analysis because in this way their results must remain universally applicable.

Thus, Professor Lange's *Price Flexibility and Employment*[4] has justly been criticized on this score, and other such examples will readily occur to the reader. That these books have made important contributions is not to be denied, but one cannot help feeling that the authors would have achieved a great deal more had they been willing to limit the applicability of their results and to commit themselves to a set of

[2]Professor Machlup seems to take the position that the valid role of generalization is to provide the analytic equipment for investigation of particular problems. See F. Machlup, "The Problem of Verification in Economics," *The Southern Economic Journal*, Vol. XXII, July 1955, pp. 2–3. If I interpret him correctly, I agree with his position on this point. For example, mathematical programming has been extremely successful in supplying tools that can be employed in the analysis of many concrete problems.

[3]See, e.g., V. Pareto, *Manuel D'Économie Politique*, 2nd ed., Paris, Girard, 1927, Ch. 1, especially pp. 7–9.

[4]Bloomington, Ind., Principia Press, 1944.

meaningful (and therefore questionable) premises.[5] Later I shall argue that the development of oligopoly theory has been retarded by the search for very general models.

3. Another alternative: realism regardless of cost

Another methodological position which differs from that taken here involves the search for ever greater realism in economic models, where the increased realism is regarded as an end in itself. Because this is so widespread an attitude, it seems almost unnecessary to provide examples. Almost all the literature criticizing the assumption of the economic man and his psychology is of this variety. Moreover, this is a viewpoint held not only by critics of the theorists but by many of the theorists themselves. How often we are presented with models whose justification is their "greater approximation to reality"[6] or a set of miscellaneous complications tacked on at the end of an analytic construct designed to increase its correspondence with "the real world."[7]

Of course, I am not opposed to realism *per se*. To oppose greater realism when it can be achieved without cost is like being against virtue. What I am arguing is that increased realism, like greater generality, usually involves a cost in decreased manipulatability and insight into the workings of our models. For one thing, when models are too complex we often find that the mathematician has not as yet supplied us with tools that are both appropriate and adequate. It often becomes necessary, therefore, to economize on the introduction of realism into our analyses.

To me, then, it is naïve to criticize a model for being unrealistic unless the cost of increased realism is taken into account. Rather, legitimate objections must assert either that in some particular case increased realism could have been introduced at a reasonable price or that the premises of the model ignore, or conflict so sharply with, the

[5]It is interesting, also, how often the authors of works written in an entirely different spirit have cited generality *per se* as a prime virtue of their approach. Thus, see J. M. Keynes, *The General Theory of Employment, Interest, and Money*, New York, Harcourt, Brace & World, 1936, p. 3, and Edward H. Chamberlin, *The Theory of Monopolistic Competition*, 7th ed., Cambridge, Mass., Harvard University Press, 1956, p. 206.

[6]See, e.g., my own "Notes on Some Dynamic Models," *Economic Journal*, Vol. LVIII, December 1948.

[7]See, e.g., R. M. Goodwin, "The Nonlinear Accelerator and the Persistence of Business Cycles," *Econometrica*, Vol. XIX, January 1951, and Baumol, *idem*. It should be clear that throughout this chapter I have sought to take my bad examples either from my own work or from works and authors whose obvious quality enables them to take care of themselves.

relevant features of the real problem that the construct is irrelevant or totally untrustworthy.

4. The Friedman position

My point of view appears to be related to Professor Friedman's methodological position. Friedman has decried the theorist whose "objective [is] a set of assumptions that [are] 'more' realistic"[8] and argues that "a theory cannot be tested by comparing its 'assumptions' directly with 'reality' ";[9] rather, "a hypothesis can be tested only by the conformity of its implications or predictions with observable phenomena."[10]

The meaning of this quotation is not fully clear to me. These statements together with some of the explanatory material in the essay can be interpreted to indicate that his position and mine have a great deal in common. On the other hand, Friedman's arguments can be taken as an injunction to look for good correlations and make no attempt to judge whether or not they are spurious.[11] If this is what he means, I must part company with him.

Even if it turns out that we do mean the same thing, I must take exception to his formulation—which may have been inspired by his penchant for the paradoxical—for in its present form it lends encouragement to irresponsible and dangerous practices by an apparent denial of the importance of the choice of assumptions. It seems to me that one of the most convenient instruments for judging the appropriateness of our necessarily imperfectly realistic models is the examination of the plausibility of their assumptions. While ridiculous premises may sometimes yield correct conclusions, we can have no confidence that they will do so.

5. Implications for development theory

To me these methodological points have suggested reasons for the varying degrees of success economists have experienced in seeking to obtain meaningful results from their researches into economic development. Let us examine some of the work on development theory in this light.

[8]"The Methodology of Positive Economics," *Essays in Positive Economics*, Chicago, University of Chicago Press, 1953, p. 32.

[9]*Ibid.*, p. 41.

[10]*Ibid.*, p. 40.

[11]But if enough predictions are made on the basis of such a relationship and they turn out to be reasonably correct, perhaps it can be presumed that the correlation is not spurious. At any rate, the model will have served a purpose. Certainly the increasing use of such tests for econometric models is highly commendable.

Recently, many writers have referred nostalgically to the classical[12] dynamic systems. In fact, many recent writings on longer run dynamic theory contain discussions of the work of the classical writers and carry the more or less explicit implication that there is much to be learned from them.[13] This suggests a fruitfulness of the classical analysis relative to modern approaches which, I would say, can to a considerable extent be ascribed to the viewpoint, the interests, and the methods of these writers. In the first place, they were concerned with concrete problems, many of which were questions of public policy. Their analyses grew out of discussions of issues like free trade (the Corn Laws discussion being a celebrated example), of problems of monetary policy in inflation (the bullion controversy), of poverty and the poor laws, and of the feasibility of utopian socialist schemes (for example, the oft-told tale of Malthus and Godwin). Let me hasten to say that the practical bent of the classical writers should not be overstated. Naturally, any such generalization about a group of different men with different temperaments and viewpoints is bound to be misleading,[14] in some degree and also, admittedly, most of them considered political economy to be much more than an art for dealing case by case with specific policy questions. They were interested in finding "economic laws"— generalizations that could help to explain, perhaps for all time, the workings of the economy.[15]

[12]I use the term very loosely to include work from the time of Adam Smith through that of J. S. Mill.

[13]See B. S. Keirstead, *The Theory of Economic Change*, Toronto, Macmillan, 1948, Ch. 4; R. F. Harrod, *Towards a Dynamic Economics*, London, Macmillan, 1948, pp. 15ff; T. Haavelmo, *A Study in the Theory of Economic Evolution*, Amsterdam, North-Holland Publishing Co., 1954, pp. 7–12; H. Leibenstein, *A Theory of Economic-Demographic Development*, Princeton, Princeton University Press, 1954, Ch. 2.

[14]"I do not apprehend, if we were in the habit of voting *aye* or *no* on the questions proposed, that there would have been half a dozen occasions since the establishment of the club, 6 years ago, in which anything like unanimity would have prevailed." J. L. Mallet, *Political Economy Club, Minutes of Proceedings*, etc., 1821–1920, p. 217, quoted in L. Robbins, *The Theory of Economic Policy in English Classical Political Economy*, London, Macmillan, 1952, p. 3, fn. 3.

[15]In this connection it is interesting to recall how Ricardo's value theory has been traced to his interest in the Corn Laws. Thus, e.g., Robbins, *op. cit.*, p. 173, and W. C. Mitchell, *Lecture Notes on Types of Economic Theory* (transcribed by a student), New York, Augustus M. Kelley, 1949, Vol. I, pp. 135–40. But Mr. Sraffa has pointed out that "By August 1813 . . . the question under discussion between Malthus and himself [Ricardo] had become the relation between the increase of capital and the rate of profits. Ricardo's letters at this time contain the essential elements of what he already calls his 'theory.' . . . At this stage, and up to March 1814, Ricardo and Malthus were not explicitly concerned with the question of the importation of corn, which had not yet aroused the public interest." *The Works and Correspondence of David Ricardo*, P. Sraffa and M. H. Dobb, eds., Cambridge, Eng., Cambridge University Press, 1951, editor's note, Vol. IV, p. 3.

Nevertheless, compared to recent work on utility theory, for example, it can be said without hesitation that the writings of the classics are "problem oriented." This becomes particularly persuasive when it is recalled that by "problems" I do not necessarily mean political questions but also concrete questions on the order of "What can be expected to happen to wages as a result of restrictions on the importation of grain?"

Second, and in my view, equally important, the classical writers were perfectly willing to go out on a limb and base their reasoning on what Samuelson has called "alleged technological and psychological laws" (to contrast them with the maximization and stability assumptions that are so much more frequently employed in recent analytic work).[16] Diminishing returns, competition, "rational behavior," and the psychological foundations of the population hypothesis are all of this variety. These are all meaningful assumptions that are certainly not universally true. But the important thing is that these assumptions seem to have been useful and relevant for their problems and their times.

However, note again that it cannot be claimed that these writers viewed such propositions in this way; rather, many of them were seeking truths of general validity and universal applicability.[17] In my opinion it is fortunate (though not fortuitous) that they failed and that in failing they developed analytic structures that resulted in a better understanding of the issues that concerned them.

I shall refer to the work of only two contemporary writers on dynamics for illustrative application of my methodological position.

In the first lecture of his volume on dynamic economics, Mr. Harrod seems to propose to do more than he is interested in performing. He appears to be seeking to produce the beginnings of an over-all dynamic theory, one that will at the same time extend the Keynesian and the classical analyses. He says, "I want to see those keen tools of thought of Pigou and Hicks ... applied to the rough dynamics of Ricardo, changing it indeed out of recognition in the process, as modern marginal analysis has already long since changed the theories of price and cost of Adam Smith and Ricardo."[18] He also tells us that, in his

[16]See P. A. Samuelson, *Foundations of Economic Analysis*, Cambridge, Mass., Harvard University Press, 1948, pp. 21–23.

[17]For example, D. Ricardo, *Principles of Political Economy and Taxation* (any edition), second and third paragraphs of the preface, and J. R. McCulloch, *Principles of Political Economy*, 4th ed., Edinburgh A. & C. Black, 1849, p. 17: "to arrive at a well-founded conclusion in this science ... we must ... inquire whether these results be constant and universally applicable, and whether the same circumstances which have given rise to them in one instance would in every instance, and in every state of society, be productive of the same or similar results."

[18]Harrod, *op. cit.*, p. 27.

use of the classics, he has dropped the population hypothesis and the law of diminishing returns[19]—again implying that he intends to amend and modernize the structure—but he ends up with a dynamic theory which, though interesting and enlightening, is not an analysis of long-run movements.

It is a short-run model applicable to cycle theory and related phenomena, and in this area it has been used. This is not surprising. His is essentially a Keynesian model, and the success of such models is, I think, in good part the result of their complete abstraction from long-run considerations. This difference from the classical analysis is well illustrated in Mr. Harrod's reminder that "In the old economics accumulation was the motive power. Here we have a stark contradiction to Keynesian doctrine in which saving is always tending to retard advance."[20] I think both views are right; each for its own problem. An analytic structure must either apply to just one of these (the long run or the short run), or it must fail to yield interesting results for this fundamental question—the role of savings in the process of change.

I believe the methodological problems of Haavelmo's recent volume[21] are rather more serious. Here my complaints are opposite to those I have just lodged against Harrod. Haavelmo begins with a most satisfactory and clear-headed description of the things he seeks in a model in the magnificent dynamics—indeed, it is so satisfactory that I shall quote it as a statement of the theme of Part II of this book. But after this promising beginning, most of Haavelmo's volume is devoted to the discussion of a long series of alternative mathematical models; and the analysis deals primarily with their formal properties rather than their relevance and economic implications. These models are presented only as examples of the limitless formal possibilities, and there is no attempt to make any single choice from among them. The results are almost necessarily empty because Haavelmo does not consider it his province to select a specific set of assumptions he believes to be reasonably valid for the analysis of the problems he has raised. Here indeed are the fruits of successful generalization.

6. Methods of this book: summary

As a consequence of my methodological position, the material in the rest of the book differs in at least one respect from many theoretical writings. This volume is characterized by the frequent appearance of

---

[19] *Ibid.*, pp. 19–20.

[20] *Ibid.*, p. 19.

[21] T. Haavelmo, *loc. cit.*

conjectures and unsupported hypotheses, some of which are at least occasionally false or highly oversimplified. These assertions are usually signaled by phrases such as "I believe" or "it is my impression that." This chapter has indicated in some detail why I engage in this procedure without apology.

To summarize, it is my view that the theorist has his choice of several approaches which, for brevity, I now caricature into two extreme types:

1. He can play it safe by working only with the few relationships of which he is reasonably sure (or pretends he is reasonably sure); for example, the allegation that businessmen seek to maximize profits. Of course, the safest propositions are tautologies (for example, the assertion that expectations must be elastic, of unit-elasticity, or inelastic), which are true by definition and can never be disproved by intractable facts. But in my view this approach, which makes its appearance in much modern economic theorizing, is of limited fruitfulness because deductions can never have more empirical content than the premises from which they are derived.

2. The alternative methodological position, that to which I adhere, asserts that theory can be more enlightening if it calls attention to empirical hypotheses whose fruitfulness is demonstrated by the implications which are deduced from them. Moreover, it will often be possible to justify the use of hypotheses that are only approximately true (and that only in a limited number of cases) in terms of the greater content of the conclusions to which they lead.

I suspect the approach that results from this methodological position and its frequent recourse to unverified conjectures will be disturbing to many readers. For this reason and because I believe the issue is so important, I have discussed this matter at some length in this chapter.

ON THE STATIC THEORY
OF OLIGOPOLY

CHAPTER 2

Introduction to part I

Perhaps the most remarkable failure of modern value theory is its inability to explain the pricing, output, and other related decisions of the large, not quite monopolistic firms that account for so high a proportion of our economy's activity. In recent years some of the greatest minds in our profession have worked on the theoretical analysis of oligopoly—with truly illuminating and revolutionary results—but, because the theory of games has set its sights so high, it has said little about the more pedestrian features of oligopolistic behavior which Part I of this volume seeks to analyze.

The definition of the term "oligopoly" as it is used in this book is relatively important. I take this designation to apply to any comparatively large company that produces commodities some of which are identical with, or very similar to, the output of other firms. There is nothing remarkable in this rather vague definition except in what it omits: it does not specify the extent to which interdependence colors the decision-making of oligopolistic firms. The idea of interactions among oligopolistic decisions, and the role this plays in the oligopolist's expectation patterns, has loomed very large in the theory. But I shall argue below that, in practice, management is often not deeply concerned with these elements of interdependence in its day-to-day decision-making. If this is not the conventional oligopolist, it is still possible that he is the giant producer, who plays so large a role in our economy. [1]

It is obvious that this shift in emphasis permits me to simplify my oligopoly model considerably, and this simplification, in turn, makes it far easier to draw definite conclusions from the resulting theory. Nevertheless, I am aware that this solution to the problem of the theoretical analysis of oligopolistic behavior is similar to the cutting

[1]One of my readers has suggested that the term "big business" might come closer to indicating my intention than does "oligopoly." It should be noted, however, that these same firms may very clearly recognize their interdependence when making major nonroutine decisions involving, for example, the introduction of a new product or of an all-out advertising campaign.

of the Gordian knot only in that both procedures ignore totally the fundamental difficulties with which other approaches to the problem have sought to cope.

Perhaps even more important for the model is a relatively novel hypothesis on oligopolistic objectives described in Chapter 6. This hypothesis, which is substituted for the usual profit maximization premise, is at best only an approximation to a set of complex and variegated facts. There seem to be no simple methods whereby it can be tested by statistical or other standard techniques of empirical investigation. Nevertheless, I do not believe that it can be rejected summarily. Indeed, it appears, on the basis of observation that was not entirely casual, to represent the facts somewhat better than some of the more usual models. In addition, as the reader shall see, this hypothesis can help to explain a number of well-known features of oligopolistic behavior that seemed puzzling until now. These are surely standard grounds of scientific method for permitting one hypothesis tentatively to supersede another.

CHAPTER 3

Oligopolistic interdependence and the multiplicity of solutions[1]

Anyone who has even a rudimentary acquaintance with the theory of oligopoly pricing (and of the making of other related decisions) must be aware of the large number of solutions that have been offered. So long as the theorist is determined that his theory shall be more or less generally valid—that is, so long as it is designed to cover all manner of possible situations—he can hope to rule out very few of these solutions.

It is also well known that oligopolistic interdependence is an important source of the difficulty. So long as the oligopolist's thought process is taken to be a compound of the form "I know that he knows that I know," we may well expect almost anything to emerge from the resulting confusion. Most of the literature has refused to go this far. It has handled the problem by assuming (explicitly or implicitly) that the executive expects his competitors to follow some specific response pattern ("If I do A he will do B"). These models then assume the firm to make decisions that are optimal only if the conjectured response structure is followed by rival concerns. The result is a number of different solutions—approximately as many as there are assumed reaction patterns.[2]

All this, as I have said, is well known. Yet it may be illuminating to examine some of the best known of these solutions. The process of

---

[1] The construction of this chapter draws heavily on J. P. Mayberry, J. F. Nash, and M. Shubik, "A Comparison of Treatments of a Duopoly Situation," *Econometrica*, Vol. XXI, January 1953. After the manuscript had been completed I also came across the same construction in H. G. Lewis, "Some Observations on Duopoly Theory," *American Economic Review, Papers and Proceedings*, Vol. XXXVIII, May 1948.

[2] Actually there are even more solutions than this would indicate since there are models whose optimal solutions are not unique. Sometimes even an infinite number of solutions (a range of values of some continuous variables) can yield results that are equally satisfactory from management's point of view.

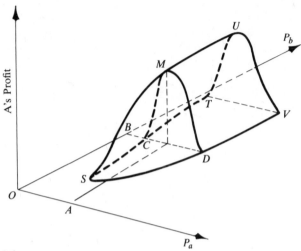

FIG. 3.1

comparison on a single diagram may help to indicate the magnitude of the oligopolist's (and the economist's) difficulties when he tries to take interdependence fully into account.

1. The duopoly payoff function

I shall discuss only the pricing decisions of two firms. The diagrams can easily be adapted to the analysis of their outputs, their advertising expenditure levels, or any other quantifiable competitive decision. Let us call the two firms A and B. In Figure 3.1 we represent A's payoff as a function of the prices that A and B have set on their products. I take these products to be somewhat different so that they need not be sold at identical prices (unlike the Bertrand case, it need not pay one duopolist to undercut the other), and I follow the usual assumption that both firms wish to maximize their own profits, so that the terms "payoff" and "profit" can be used interchangeably.

The diagram indicates that, given his own price, A's profit will increase when there is a rise in the price that B charges for his product. This is shown by the rise in A's profit surface $STUV$ as we move toward the rear of the diagram. With rising prices, B gradually prices himself out of the market. A's payoff surface levels off after B's product becomes so expensive that no one will buy it; so further rises in B's price can add nothing more to A's sales.

The figure also shows (the upside down U-shaped cross sections perpendicular to the P_b axis, such as CMD) that for any given price of

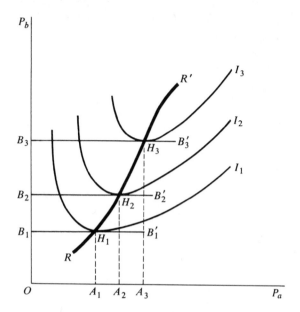

FIG. 3.2

B's product, for example, OB, there is a profit maximizing price OA (for A) so prices lower or higher than this reduce A's profits.

Figure 3.2 shows the corresponding profit indifference curves for A (the curves labeled I). From Figure 3.1 we see that these curves, which are projections of the intersections of surface $STUV$ with horizontal planes of various heights, must be U shaped. The positively sloping segments indicate that an excessive rise in A's price can be prevented from reducing his profits only by a simultaneous increase in B's price. By assumption, it will pay A to get on as high an indifference curve as possible because higher curves in Figure 3.2 correspond to larger profits.

2. The Cournot solution

We can now use this diagram to describe what has come to be called the Cournot solution.[3] Consider A's optimal response to any fixed price, say, OB_3, for B's product. It will pay A to set his price at OA_3, for then he will have attained the highest profit indifference curve compatible with B's price. He will be at the point of tangency H_3 between one of his

---

[3]Cournot himself deals with the determination of *output* levels for identical products. Instead, I have discussed *pricing*, partly because the exposition is somewhat easier and partly to show that a similar analysis applies in this case.

indifference curves I_3 and the horizontal line B_3B_3', along which B's price has the given value.

In the same way, we find that A's optimal response to a fixed price OB_2 for product B is to choose price OA_2 for his own product (point of tangency H_2), etc. The locus of all those points of tangency—which is obviously the locus of all points at which A's profit indifference curves are horizontal—is curve RR'. This is A's price reaction curve: It shows A's optimal price response to each possible price level set by B.[4]

In a similar manner, we can draw in B's profit indifference curves (the broken J curves in Figure 3.3a) and then B's price reaction curve SS', which is the locus of all points, such as V_3 and V_4, at which his profit indifference curves are vertical.

The curves RR' and SS' have one point, C, the Cournot equilibrium point, in common. This point has the property that any other point

FIG. 3.3A

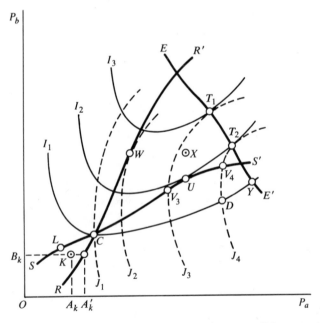

[4]The positive slope of RR' suggests that the two commodities are substitutes, that is, a rise in the price of B shifts upward the demand curve for A's product, and induces A to raise his price. However, substitutability is neither necessary nor sufficient for such a slope because even when the demand curve shifts upward, if its elasticity increases sufficiently at the same time, it will pay to cut price.

must represent a price combination, which either A or B or both will want to change if they behave in accord with their reaction curves. Thus (Figure 3.3a), starting from, for example, point K, A will want to increase his price from OA_k to OA'_k because B's price starts out at OB_k and, similarly, B will want to raise his price. Hence, K cannot represent a stable situation under the implicit Cournot assumption, which will be recalled in a moment. The same holds true at any other point in the diagram except C.[5] There is no need to recapitulate the simple dynamic process that has been taken to lead the competitors toward point C[6].

3. More sophisticated alternatives: breakdown of the solution process

It is more important for our present purposes to recall that the model has implicitly taken each competitor to believe his rival's price to be

FIG. 3.3B

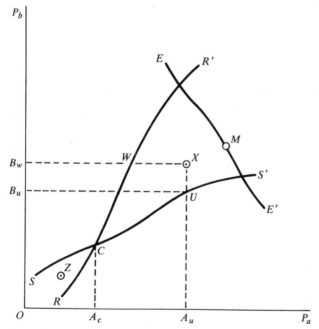

[5]At a point like L, which lies on one of the price reaction curves, only one of the competitors will want to change his price—but that is enough to prevent it from being an equilibrium point.

[6]See A. A. Cournot, *Researches into the Mathematical Principles of the Theory of Wealth*, N. T. Bacon, trans., New York, Macmillan, 1897, Ch. 7, especially Fig. 2, for the (first order nonlinear difference equation) model.

fixed.[7] That is the meaning of the horizontal price level lines BB' in Figure 3.2. The price reaction curve represents A's optimal response to alternative prices of B only if the latter are fixed and immutable.

Once A recognizes that B will respond to his own price changes (A certainly must notice this, if they both grope gradually toward point C), he will no longer have any motivation to settle on his own reaction curve. At the Cournot equilibrium point he is on profit indifference curve I_1 (Figure 3.3a), but by increasing his price from OA_c to OA_u (Figure 3.3b), if B responds in accord with his reaction curve, the price combination will move from that represented by point C to that indicated by U. A is now on a higher indifference curve than he was before (Figure 3.3a). In fact, he has attained the highest indifference curve compatible with B's reaction curve SS', because I_2 is tangent to SS' at U.[8]

But B can reason in precisely the same way, and instead of raising his price to OB_u in order to remain on his reaction curve, he can set it[9] at level OB_w (Figure 3.3b) in the hope that he will attain point W, at which one of his indifference curves is tangent to A's reaction curve (Figure 3.3a).

With A's price at level OA_u and B's at OB_w, neither point W nor point U will represent the results: Rather, both firms will be surprised to end up instead at point X, where (as in the case drawn in the diagram) they may[10] even be delighted to find they are both on higher profit indifference curves than they had expected.

But even if they are pleased, neither oligopolist has any motivation to try to remain at point X. For there they each learn that the other has abandoned his reaction curve altogether, and his calculation of the other's response pattern and his own search for optimal countermoves

---

[7]Cf. E. H. Chamberlin, *The Theory of Monopolistic Competition*, 7th ed., Cambridge, Mass., Harvard University Press, 1956, pp. 32–34. It is to be remembered that since Professor Chamberlin deals with the strict Cournot case where quantity rather than price is the decision variable, he points out that the Cournot model has each oligopolist assuming his rival's *supply* constant.

[8]The move from C to U must involve an increase in the prices of both products so long as SS' has a positive slope—for SS' intersects I_1 where it is horizontal at point C (Fig. 3.3a). Hence, all points on the segment of SS' that lie to the left of C must lie on lower indifference curves. Only by moving upward and to the right from C along SS' can A increase its profits.

[9]Note that OB_w may or may not be higher than OB_u, as a little shifting of the indifference curves in Fig. 3.3a will show.

[10]If, e.g., OB_w is below OB_u (see preceding footnote), it is no longer true that both parties will find X better than they had expected.

must begin afresh. The entire Cournot solution structure will have broken down and our analysis is back where it began—at the infinite sequence of guesses and counterguesses.

4. The Edgeworth contract curve

An alternative approach to the entire matter is to assume that the duopolists will end up somewhere on the Edgeworth contract curve. This curve is the locus of points at which A's and B's indifference curves are tangent (that is, points T_1 and T_2 in Figure 3.3a). It is drawn in as curve EE' (Figures 3.3).[11]

The argument for this solution is that, starting at any point not on the contract curve, it is possible for both oligopolists to change their prices in a manner that is mutually advantageous. For example, any point inside segment $T_2 Y$ of the contract curve puts both A and B on higher indifference curves than when they are at point D in Figure 3.3a.

But it does not follow that both firms will want to change when they are at a point off the contract curve. So long as each feels up in the air about what the other is going to do, he can have no assurance that a move to the contract curve will put him in a sector of the curve on which he is better off. Thus, at point U off the curve, A is better off than he would be at point Y on EE', and if he starts out feeling settled at U, he may simply prefer not to reopen the price adjustment process for fear that it may do him no good. Indeed, the same possibility applies to any point in the diagram at which neither firm is losing money. *Thus, any such point can turn out to be a point of equilibrium.*

However, its stability may well be doubted, for from any point it is possible to move in a way advantageous to at least one player. If such a change occurs accidentally, it is difficult to see why the original situation should be returned to, unless the other player suffers a loss and succeeds in cowing his rival by a threat to engage in price policies that perhaps can be ruinous to both. And even then they may settle on another compromise point. The analysis is still totally up in the air.

[11]It is no accident of drawing that places the Cournot equilibrium point C off the contract curve EE', for at C the reaction curves intersect and so A's indifference curve I_1 must be horizontal there and B's indifference curve J_1, at that point, must be vertical. Therefore, the two indifference curves can never be tangent at point C. For an earlier statement of the geometric argument see H. G. Lewis, *loc. cit.* A proof for the N firm homogeneous oligopoly industry is given in Mathematical Note a at the end of this chapter.

There will be another locus of such points of tangency that lies below C and represents price combinations from which any change must benefit at least one player.

5. Other suggested equilibria

In these confused circumstances, it is to be expected that other alternative possibilities should have been considered.

The number of these alternative suggestions is so large that any attempt at a survey would be a major task from which little is to be gained. I mention only a few outstanding cases:

Neumann and Morgenstern have suggested that the firms will first maximize their joint profits and only then battle between themselves over the division of the spoils.[12] This would put the price combination at some *unique*[13] point *M* on the contract curve (Figure 3.3b), because that curve is the locus of *all* points from which any change must be to the disadvantage of one player. The precise location of *M* cannot be determined unless the levels of profit associated with each of the *I* and *J* indifference curves is specified so we can determine at which point on *EE'* the total of these profits is maximized. *M*, of course, is the monopoly equilibrium point; that is, it represents the prices which would be charged if both outputs were sold by a single profit maximizing firm. This solution was also proposed by A. A. Young and by Schumpeter.[14]

The zero-profit competitive price combination (a point *Z* which usually lies below and to the left of the Cournot point *C*) has also been suggested.[15]

Alternative solutions have also been proposed by Bertrand, Pareto, Von Stackelberg, Sweezy, Fellner,[16] Nash,[17] and others.

In view of the discussion of the preceding section, the length of the list of these alternatives is hardly surprising. Nor can it be cut down

[12]*Theory of Games and Economic Behavior*, Princeton, Princeton University Press, 1947, 2nd ed., p. 513.

[13]It is the uniqueness of the Neumann-Morgenstern point that distinguishes the representation of their solution from that of Edgeworth, which includes as possibilities all points on an arc of the contract curve. The indeterminacy which nevertheless characterizes the Neumann-Morgenstern solution in this nonzero sum case only involves the magnitudes of the side payments required to get the players to point *M*.

[14]See Chamberlin, *op. cit.* p. 47, fn. 2, and p. 50.

[15]*Ibid.*, pp. 43 and 48–49. The latter refers only to the case where the number of oligopolists is fairly large. See also pp. 32–34 and 221–22 for a restatement of Cournot's argument that his prices will exceed the zero profit levels so that *C* will lie above and to the right of *Z*. For a discussion of an error in the original Cournot argument, see Mathematical Note b at the end of this chapter.

[16]For references and discussion see Chamberlin, *op. cit.* Ch. 3, Appendix A, and the bibliography, William Fellner, *Competition Among the Few*, New York, Knopf, 1949, especially Chs. 2, 3, and 6, and F. Machlup, *The Economics of Sellers' Competition*, Baltimore, Johns Hopkins, 1952, especially Parts V and VI.

[17]See Mayberry, Nash, and Shubik, *loc. cit.*

without some sort of empirical evidence, for each point can be made the correct solution of some appropriately constructed model. For example, any point Q (not shown in the diagram) will be the equilibrium point in a model in which each player conjectures that the other's behavior will follow a (not necessarily Cournot variety) reaction curve that is tangent to one of his own indifference curves at point Q.

In the next chapter, and in Chapter 6, I propose to follow a new course: to present some fragmentary empirical observations that can provide the basis for a stable oligopoly value theory, which, in turn, seems to offer explanations of phenomena that have been observed in other areas, as well as a determinate price and output pattern.

MATHEMATICAL NOTES

a. The Cournot equilibrium point and the contract locus

In this chapter it has been proved diagrammatically that in the duopoly case the Cournot equilibrium point will *never* lie on the contract curve (see footnote 11, above). The theorem will now be generalized to the case of the N firm homogeneous product[18] oligopoly industry.

The profit function of firm i is given by

(3.1) $T_i = P(Q_1 + \cdots + Q_N)Q_i - C_i(Q_i)$

where $P(Q_1 + \cdots + Q_N)$ is the industry's price expressed as a function of total industry output (the demand function); Q_i is the output of firm i; and $C_i(Q_i)$ is its total cost function. The Cournot equilibrium point is given by the N simultaneous equations

(3.2) $T_{ii} \equiv \partial T_i/\partial Q_i = 0 \qquad i = 1, \ldots, N.$

On the other hand the locus of the contract curve is found by solving the following maximization problem:

Maximize the first firm's profit, T_1, subject to the condition that all other firms' profits are given:

$$T_2 = K_2, T_3 = K_3, \ldots, T_N = K_N$$

where the K's are constants. That is, the contract curve is the locus of all points which yield maximum profits to any one firm for any given

[18]C. E. Ferguson has shown, however, that if the firms in the industry differentiate their products the Cournot point can lie on the contract curve. Thus, my more general claim in the first edition of this book was incorrect. See Ferguson's "Cournot Points and the Conflict Curves," *Review of Economic Studies*, Vol. XXIX, February 1962.

level of profits for each of the other firms. Necessary Lagrangian conditions for such a maximum are

(3.3) $T_{1j} + \lambda_2 T_{2j} + \cdots + \lambda_N T_{Nj} = 0 \qquad j = 1, \ldots, N$

where the λ's are Lagrange multipliers and T_{ij} represents $\partial T_i / \partial Q_j$. Differentiation of the profit function (3.1) yields, for any $i \neq j$,

$$T_{ij} = P' Q_i$$

where $P' = dP/d\Sigma Q_i = dP/dQ_i$ for all i. Let us set $T_{ii} = 0$ for every firm $i = 1, \ldots, N$ in accord with the requirements (3.2) of the Cournot equilibrium, and substitute this and $T_{ij} = P' Q_i$ into the Lagrangian contract curve equations (3.3) above to see if the resulting system can be solved, that is, to see whether the Cournot conditions (3.2) are consistent with the contract curve equations (3.3). We obtain

(3.4)
$$
\begin{aligned}
0 + P' Q_2 \lambda_2 + P' Q_3 \lambda_3 + \cdots + P' Q_N \lambda_N &= 0 \\
P' Q_1 + 0 \quad\quad + P' Q_3 \lambda_3 + \cdots + P' Q_N \lambda_N &= 0 \\
\cdots\cdots\cdots\cdots\cdots\cdots\cdots\cdots\cdots\cdots\cdots \\
P' Q_1 + P' Q_2 \lambda_2 + P' Q_3 \lambda_3 + \cdots + 0 \quad\quad &= 0
\end{aligned}
$$

which is a system of homogeneous linear equations in the variables $Q_1, Q_2\lambda_2, \ldots, Q_N\lambda_N$. This system has a solution other than the trivial universal zero output solution $Q_1 = \cdots = Q_N\lambda_N = 0$ if and only if the matrix of the system is singular.[19] After canceling out the P''s we see that the determinant is

$$
\begin{vmatrix}
0 & 1 & \cdots & 1 \\
1 & 0 & \cdots & 1 \\
\cdots\cdots\cdots\cdots \\
1 & 1 & \cdots & 0
\end{vmatrix}.
$$

Subtracting the first row from all of the others we obtain

$$
\begin{vmatrix}
0 & 1 & 1 & \cdots & 1 \\
1 & -1 & 0 & \cdots & 0 \\
1 & 0 & -1 & \cdots & 0 \\
\cdots\cdots\cdots\cdots\cdots\cdots \\
1 & 0 & 0 & \cdots & -1
\end{vmatrix}
$$

that is, a determinant with zero in the upper left-hand corner, minus ones in the rest of the principal diagonal, unit elements in the rest of

[19]Harold Kuhn has pointed out that one can proceed in a somewhat simpler manner from this point and avoid the use of determinants. To prove that (3.4) yields $Q_1 = 0$, we multiply the first equation through by $(N - 2)$ and subtract it from the sum of the other equations to obtain directly $(N - 1)Q_1 = 0$. Obviously we can do the same for each of the remaining Q_i in turn.

the first row and column, and zeros elsewhere. Adding all of the rows successively to the first, the determinant becomes

$$\begin{vmatrix} N & 0 & 0 & \cdots & 0 \\ 1 & -1 & 0 & \cdots & 0 \\ 1 & 0 & -1 & \cdots & 0 \\ \cdots & \cdots & \cdots & \cdots & \cdots \\ 1 & 0 & 0 & \cdots & -1 \end{vmatrix} = N(-1)^{N-1} \neq 0.$$

Hence, the system of homogeneous equations (3.4) obtained from Cournot equations (3.2) and the contract curve equations (3.3) has no nonzero solution, and so the Cournot equilibrium point cannot satisfy the conditions which trace out the contract curve.

b. *An error in Cournot's argument*

Cournot states[20] that even if the demand curve is nonlinear, an increase in the number of oligopolists must, in his model, always reduce price (see footnote 15 above). Unfortunately, the argument seems to have a

FIG. 3.4

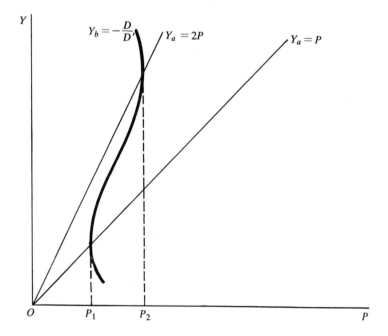

[20]*Op. cit.*, pp. 82–84.

mathematical flaw, though the statement is nevertheless true at least in the simple zero cost case if the second-order maximum conditions are valid.

Cournot deduces from the equilibrium conditions in his model the equation $-D/D' = NP$, where D is the quantity demanded from all firms in the industry, $D' \equiv dD/dP$, P is the price of the product, and N is the number of oligopolists who constitute the industry. Cournot maintains that this equation shows (despite the fact that both D and D' are functions of P) that P must vary inversely with N. His argument is that the solution of the equation is given by the intersection of the graph of the line $Y_a = NP$ with the curve $Y_b = -D/D'$ (represented as a function of P). Because the slope of the curve $Y_a = NP$ is equal to N, Cournot states that if the value of Y_b is real and positive for every value of P, the intersection of the graph of Y_b with that of Y_a must move toward the left (smaller values of P) as N increases.

Figure 3.4 shows that this is not the case. If the slope of $-D/D'$ is greater than N (and hence also positive), the intersection of the Y_b curve with $Y_a = NP$ must occur to the right of its intersection with $Y_a = (N-1)P$, and the price P_N in an N firm Cournot industry will be higher than it would be with $N-1$ firms. Thus, in the diagram $P_2 > P_1$.

The condition for this peculiar case to arise is clearly

(3.5) $$\frac{dY_b}{dP} = \frac{d(-D/D')}{dP} > N = \frac{dY_a}{dP}.$$

However, the Cournot result can be derived in a different manner.[21] Suppose the second-order conditions hold throughout for the profit function of every firm. For any such firm, i, to maximize its profits we must have

$$d(D_iP)/dD_i = P + D_iP' = 0$$

and, by the second-order conditions,

$$d(P + D_iP')/dD_i = \frac{d(P + D_iP')}{dP} \frac{dP}{dD_i} < 0,$$

that is,

$$d(P + D_iP')/dP = 1 + d(D_iP')/dP > 0.$$

Summing over all N firms we obtain (because $1/D' = dP/dD = P'$)

$$N > d(-D/D')/dP.$$

Thus, (3.5) cannot hold and the Cournot result follows.

[21] This was first pointed out to me by C. E. Ferguson in a letter dated January 27, 1960. Subsequently, my error was also noted by James Burtle.

CHAPTER 4

On oligopolistic interdependence in practice

Before turning to the substantive material of this brief chapter, it is necessary to explain the limitations of the evidence on which its allegations, and some of those which occur later (particularly in Chapter 6), are based. Essentially, the assertions are no more than impressions gathered through casual observation of the operation of a number of business firms.[1] In my work I have had occasion to examine in detail some of their decisions and the data on which they were based. Perhaps equally illuminating have been management's reactions to our own recommendations. These reactions certainly seemed indicative of the nature of management's objectives and, in particular, its attitude toward profit maximization. As we shall see, this will play an important part in the sequel.

It must be emphasized, then, that the empirical observations reported here were highly unsystematic and represent a sample that, as statistical studies go, must be considered extremely small. Their only and peculiar virtue is that they can lay claim to having come, as it were, from the inside.

Let us turn now to the real matter of this chapter. As we have seen in the preceding chapter, oligopolistic interdependence and the resulting difficulty in predicting competitive reactions to a decision by one of the firms in the group have rendered determinate solutions to oligopoly models particularly hard to come by. Theoretical analysis has sought to deal with this difficulty through a variety of alternative approaches that we may usefully classify into four general categories in terms of the type of assumption employed:

[1] I am extremely fortunate to have worked for several years with the firm of Alderson Associates, Inc., management and market consultants in Philadelphia, and subsequently with Mathematica, Inc., in Princeton. This gave me access to detailed information about the operations of many firms ranging from enterprises which gross as little as $2 million a year to some of the giants of industry.

1. The *fixed behavior pattern* premise in which the firms's rivals are assumed always to react predictably in accord with some clearly foreseen functional relationship. This type of premise perhaps has been the most popular among economic theorists, and the reaction curve analysis described in the preceding chapter is a prime illustration. We saw there what sorts of difficulties this sort of assumption can produce.

2. The *accommodating reaction* premise, which is a special case of the preceding approach. One assumes that, where possible, each competitor responds to another's moves in a way that is mutually advantageous. This premise provides the basis of the contract curve analysis and sometimes leads to implicit collusion models in which oligopolists are taken always to arrive at the monopolistic solution. Though this way of looking at the problem sometimes can be instructive, like each of the other alternatives, it does not seem to account for a variety of phenomena that have been observed. While it is in accord with such institutions as price leadership, it does not explain such manifestations as the instability of some cartels, the occasional price war, and, most important, the rule-of-thumb decision procedure that rarely takes explicit account of effects on the welfare of one's competition.

3. The *preparation against the worst contingency* premise—this is the maximin approach of game theory in which management is assumed to take decisions that minimize the damage that can result from the acts of rivals. In effect, the firm makes perfectly rational plans on the assumption that its competitors will behave similarly. Analytically, this is clearly a far more satisfying premise than that provided by an arbitrarily selected reaction pattern, and it has served as the basis for a rich and fruitful body of theory. Yet no one has claimed that it accords closely with the facts, and so, for descriptive analysis, the search for acceptable alternatives has continued. We come, finally, to the approach of this book.

4. The assumption *interdependence ignored in some types of decision.* I shall take the position that in *day-to-day decision-making*, management often acts explicitly or implicitly on the premise that its decisions will produce no changes in the behavior of those with whom they are competing. It is noteworthy that most pieces of advice for which the operations researcher has received credit have proceeded on this basis despite the fact that it is only the large oligopoly firm that has generally been able to afford his services. Inventory control calculations, transportation analyses, programming investigations of product line simplification, and all the other standard types of operations research have rarely made any attempt to deal with reactions of business rivals and their effects despite the mathematical sophistication the studies have

sometimes utilized. The fact that businessmen have been prepared to pay attention to this sort of reasoning suggests that it may not always be foreign to their way of thinking.

Of course, I am not arguing that management inhabits a fool's paradise in which interdependence is never considered. In making its more radical decisions, such as the launching of a major advertising campaign or the introduction of a radically new line of products, management usually does consider the probable competitive response. But often, even in fairly crucial decisions, and almost always in routine policy-making, only the most cursory attention is paid to competitive reactions. This apparently dangerous attitude does not usually lead the business-man into serious difficulty because, I believe, his more ordinary decisions are rarely met by prompt aggressive countermoves of the sort envisaged in many of our models. There are several reasons why this should be so.

1. Complexity of internal organization

The modern industrial giant is a mammoth organization almost always engaged in many activities—some of them highly diverse in character. Its great size and complexity have been accompanied by a correspond-ingly large and involved managerial organization. Proposals are char-acteristically inaugurated at points in the organization far removed from the makers of the final decisions. Moreover, because of the multiplicity of departments usually involved, and the uneasy truce between highly centralized control and departmental autonomy, responsibility is frequently divided and is rarely well defined. As a result, decision-mak-ing is often a lengthy process whose outcome is fairly unpredictable.

This decision-making apparatus is too clumsy and slow-moving for effective interplay of strategy and counterstrategy among competing firms. A move by one of them, *provided it is not too radical*, may just be ignored by the others, simply because divided responsibility invites each decision-maker to shift the responsibility onto others. Even if some countermove is proposed the suggestion is likely to be watered down as it passes through various echelons and committee meetings. What finally does come through is very likely to come only after a very considerable lapse of time.

2. The use of rules of thumb

Top executives are usually too busy, and their computational skills are sometimes too limited for them to be able to probe very deeply into every business problem. Management's difficulty is that it must retain some measure of control over the operations of the firm without, at the same time, tying itself up in operational detail. This problem is solved by the frequent use of rules of thumb—prices are set by applying a standard mark-up to costs; advertising expenditures are determined by setting aside a fixed percentage of total revenues; and inventories are required to meet a preset turnover norm.[2]

These rules of thumb do not work out too badly. They translate hopelessly involved problems into simple, orderly routines. They save executive time and permit a degree of centralized control over the firm's far-flung operations. By and large, they probably contribute considerably to over-all operating efficiency. Most executives appear to recognize these rules for what they are—imperfect expedients designed to cope, in a rough and ready manner, with a difficult control and decision problem.

But rules of thumb tend to reduce competitive give and take among oligopolistic enterprises. Because they must be relatively simple in order to be useful, these rules do not make provision for a variety of contingencies. For example, an average cost pricing rule takes no explicit account of recent trends in the decision patterns of other firms in the industry. It provides no elaborate directions for adaptation to each of the many possible moves of competitors.

In one rather typical case, the manufacturer of a fuel kept his price just slightly above that of the nearest competing fuel because his large overheads made his average cost rather high. When it was pointed out to him that a lower price could reduce his average costs substantially through an increase in his sales volume, he accepted the suggestion with apparently little concern for the possibility that his rival would retaliate by also cutting his price. Moreover, his confidence seems to have been justified by the results. It should be added that in this industry firms in many other cities seem to have had the same experience. Very likely, the manufacturers of the competing fuels failed to meet these price cuts because they too were using average cost pricing procedures.

[2]"In an oligopolistic situation, with its precarious internal equilibrium, there is much to be gained from simple and widely understood rules of thumb, which minimize the danger of behavior intended to be peaceful and cooperative being misunderstood as predatory or retaliatory . . . the experience of those who, like myself, have conducted extensive personal interviews with executives suggests that these respondents have a strong propensity to explain their behavior in terms of simple mechanical principles." F. Modigliani, "New Developments on the Oligopoly Front," *Journal of Political Economy*, Vol. LXVI, June 1958, p. 226. See also P. Sylos-Labini, *Oligopoly and Technical Progress*, Cambridge, Mass., Harvard University Press, 1962.

3. Desire for the quiet life

In recent years the managers of large firms have displayed signs of a desire for respectability and security. To avoid difficulties with public regulatory authorities as well as with their own stockholders, managements have veered away from the rough and tumble. But firms who wish to live and let live are not likely to be anxious to make life unpredictable for one another. And it is my impression that business organizations have, to some extent, come to depend on each other to be well-behaved. In fact, they frequently seem to expect others to go along with their decisions and, if anything, to adjust their policies in a cooperative spirit.[3] In some cases I have seen even the possibility of competitive counter-moves considered as a sort of breach of etiquette—as a slightly shocking contingency.

4. Reservations

In making a case of this sort it is quite easy to exaggerate and, no doubt, I have somewhat overstated the point. It is not true that a reign of perfect and universal mutual inattention has descended upon our oligopolies. Among many firms there are unsettled border disputes that lead to occasional forays. For example, in one industry where pricing seems otherwise to be conducted on a gentlemanly basis, there is mutual suspicion of the discounts that are offered (for advertising purposes) for the use of their products by nonprofit organizations! One firm undertook a sort of cloak-and-dagger investigation to find out what rebates were really being offered and indicated that it was prepared to do whatever was necessary to get its products displayed through this channel.

Moreover, it must be recognized that while it does not usually consist of a series of strategic moves and quick responses, vigorous competitive activity does take place. The oligopolist has a fiercely tender regard for his share of the market and, if ever he finds himself losing out, energetic steps may be expected. I will discuss some implications of this attitude later in the book. But for the moment I simply take note of its existence and reassert my belief that in its day-to-day pricing and output decisions, the oligopolistic firm nevertheless takes only the most cursory glance at the probable reactions of its competitors in the

---

[3]However, as has already been noted, this is quite different from a complete absence of competitive response. In practice, the outcome is usually some sort of compromise between no reaction and an accommodating response.

confident expectation that their unresponsiveness (so long as there is no large change in market share) will continue very similar to its own.

It must be emphasized that there still remains a very important role to be played by the theory of oligopolistic interdependence and its analysis with the aid of tools like those provided by game theory. For decisions relating to radical changes in policy, interdependence is usually as important as our theory has always supposed. However, the ordinary problems of value theory, the routine pricing and advertising decisions, are generally not beset by these complications. This has been the burden of the argument of this chapter. Since the remainder of Part I of this book is concerned with just such problems of value theory, no more will be said about questions of interdependence until Part II.

5. The logic of oligopolistic decision-making

If interdependence is demoted from its central role in the theory of oligopoly, some alternative must be chosen to replace it. The obvious candidate is the premise that each firm tries to maximize its profits as though it were in isolation.

However, the consequences of such an assumption are not particularly satisfying. As I shall point out later, it leaves unexplained some frequently noted features of oligopolistic behavior. Moreover, my experience, and apparently that of some others who have worked with business firms, is that profits do not constitute the prime objective of the large modern business enterprise. It must be made clear that I am not trying to reopen the tired and tiresome argument against the economic man. Surely, he never existed and does not now, but he is still a very useful approximation. On the contrary, I believe the businessman can usefully be viewed as a calculating individual, but one whose calculations take account of profits in a manner that differs somewhat from the standard view.

An alternative is to follow Simon's suggestion and assume that the firm does not maximize anything.[4] Instead, because knowledge is so imperfect and so costly to acquire, management may often rest content with a level of achievement that it considers viable and acceptable—it "satisfices" rather than attempting to maximize. No doubt there is some truth in this view, as the widespread reliance on rules of thumb so strongly suggests. Yet this picture, which may be valid enough for some purposes, does not seem to capture the very real striving for preeminence that characterizes so much of business behavior. Moreover, so far it has

[4]See, e.g., H. A. Simon, "Theories of Decision-Making in Economics," *American Economic Review*, Vol. XLIX, June 1959.

yielded no theory that is tractable analytically—one that has been able to provide interesting and meaningful theorems about the behavior of the firm.

Instead, I shall proceed on the alternative assumption that management does try to make optimal decisions, but that the size of the firm's operations shares with profits the role of prime objective—a premise I believe fits the observed facts reasonably well. For the moment I shall say no more about this hypothesis, postponing my discussion until Chapter 6. But first, to lay the ground for some of the later analysis, and to help supply plausibility to my hypothesis, I shall argue in the next chapter that even to the profit maximizing firm the scale of its operation can become an important proximate objective.

CHAPTER 5

Funds limitations and profits

1. Line of credit and other funds limitations[1]

This chapter offers an analysis of the relationship between the volume of the funds available to a firm and the profits it can expect to earn. I shall argue that, at least up to a point, increased money capital will not only increase the total profits of the firm, but because it puts the firm in a higher echelon of imperfectly competing capital groups, it may very well also increase its earnings per dollar of investment even in the long run, after all appropriate capital movements are completed.[2] It follows that businessmen may want to accumulate assets (money capital) not only for their own sake, but also as a means to increase their profit rate.

Firms obtain their funds from a variety of sources: they can plow profits back into the firm; they can sell securities[3] or borrow from the banks. None of these sources will ordinarily provide unlimited amounts of money capital to any single firm. At any given time the firm is often acutely aware that there is an upper limit to the funds available to it.

[1]This chapter is a revision of my "Firms with Limited Money Capital," *Kyklos*, Vol. VI, Fasc. II, 1953. The reader may wish to compare Mr. Hahn's "A Note On Profit and Uncertainty," *Economica*, Vol. XIV, New Series, August 1947, J. Steindl's *Small and Big Business*, Oxford, Blackwell, 1945, especially pp. 5–21, and the same author's "Capitalist Enterprise and Risk," *Oxford Economic Papers*, No. 7, March 1945. The problem has also received incidental mention in various connections, e.g., the Ricardo-effect discussion. See Sho-Chieh Tsiang, *The Variations of Real Wages and Profit Margins in Relation to the Trade Cycle*, London, Pitman, 1947, Chapter 7, for a summary and further references. *Cf.* also A. G. Hart, *Anticipations, Uncertainty and Dynamic Planning*, New York, Augustus M. Kelly, 1951, especially Chapter 3.

[2]This is contrary to received doctrine which (while admitting that in the short run larger amounts of capital may yield larger profits because they permit the firm to take advantage of economies of large-scale production, etc.) asserts that, soon, flows of capital into particularly profitable areas or scales of operation will tend to equalize all rates of return.

[3]In this chapter I shall say nothing about the role and the motivations of the stockholder. However, I shall return to this subject later.

Even during the postwar period of easy money, several firms whose operations I examined seemed to fear excess inventory at least partly because stocks tie up liquid capital and, even more important, because large inventories might have led their banks to tighten the company's line of credit.

The magnitude of the firm's own accumulation affects the amount it can borrow. An increase in its own funds makes it easier to get money elsewhere. Wealth attracts wealth, and so some firms find themselves more richly endowed with money capital than others. I will argue that this divides them into imperfectly competing groups among which there is occasional migration by merger, or by other means of combining small capital stocks into large ones.

In this discussion I shall employ four definitions:

1. *The average cost of borrowing for a firm* is used as a synonym for the "average cost of capital" of the literature of corporation finance. It is normally higher than the rate of interest on company debt because of the risk involved in the firm's overall investments, a risk from which lenders to the company are partially protected by having first claim on company earnings and assets.

2. The *size of a firm* is measured by the amount of owned and borrowed money capital invested in either liquid or illiquid form.

3. *Gross* and *net profits* (total, average, and marginal) are profits respectively gross and net of the cost of the company's capital. Here profits are considered a function of the firm's money capital. For example, *average gross profits* are defined as total profits divided by the size of the investment in the firm. Unless otherwise specified, these concepts refer to the greatest profits the entrepreneur can earn with his capital in any industry.

4. A *specific investment profit function* refers to the average gross profits the firm can obtain by investing in some specified industry. This can be obtained by subtracting average cost from average revenue for each possible size of firm.

2. Monotonicity of the gross profit curve

We note, first, that large capital holding firms have the option of competing with smaller enterprises, but the smaller firms cannot always reciprocate. The large capital holder has a choice between investing in a chain of small local movie houses or in a large, centrally located theater like New York's Radio City Music Hall. If the former alternative is the more profitable, he can invade the domain of the small exhibitor unless patrons show special favor to local small businessmen, but the neighbor-

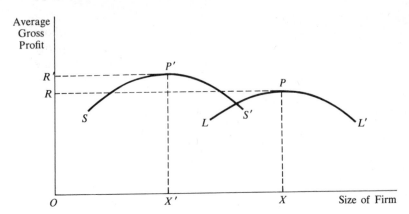

FIG. 5.1

hood theater owner, on the other hand, cannot enter the big exhibitor's province even if the profit rate dwarfs his own earnings. It follows that, other things being equal, the large firm can ordinarily obtain gross profits at least as large, and perhaps larger, than the smaller enterprise.[4]

To explain this point, suppose, to begin with, that it were not so; we will see how profits will then be driven into line by capital flows. In Figure 5.1 let SS' and LL' be the specific investment profit curves in two industries S and L. Small plants are well adapted to the needs of S and large plants to those of L. This is shown by the relative position of the peaks of the two curves—the peak P' of SS' lies to the left of the peak P of LL'. Thus, SS' may represent the opportunity to invest in a neighborhood theater etc. The way the figure is drawn, larger per-dollar returns can be earned in industry S. This contradicts the conclusion of the preceding paragraph, that larger firms can earn greater profits, but in the long run such a situation cannot persist, as it will pay an investor in industry L to move into industry S. Thus, if he has OX invested in L it will pay him to withdraw it and operate two plants of size $OX' = \frac{1}{2}OX$ in industry S. His total profits will thereby be raised from $OXPR$ to

$$2OX'P'R' = 2(OX')OR'$$
$$= (OX)(OR') > (OX)(OR) = OXPR.$$

Thus, if capital is at all mobile, funds will tend to flow from industry L to industry S. This flow of capital out of L will reduce its output and

[4]Of course, the very scale of operation of a large firm affects, and often adds to, its administrative costs so that other things cannot be equal. This may be one of the most important disadvantages of bigness to the firm working in the opposite direction

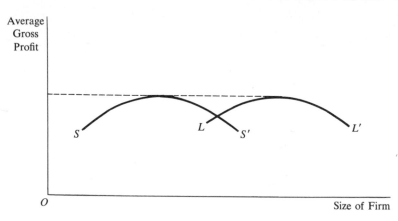

FIG. 5.2

thereby increase its prices and profits; the reverse will take place in S. Therefore, there will be an upward shift in LL' (larger profits at each firm size) and a downward shift in SS'. Precisely how high LL' will end up relative to SS' depends on the demand functions for the products of the two industries, but if the demand schedule for the product of industry L is sufficiently high to keep it from going out of business altogether, the peak of LL' will tend to be driven at least as high as the peak of SS', as is shown in Figure 5.2. Otherwise, still further capital transfers will be profitable.

It also may be expected that in contrast with the situation depicted in Figure 5.1, some industries initially will yield peculiarly high returns to large plants. Let KK' be the specific investment profit curve of such an industry (Figure 5.3), and for purposes of comparison, the diagram also contains the corresponding curve for industry S. Small investors will not be able to shift to the more profitable of the two industries as the large investors shifted their capital before. There need be no tendency in this case for the two curves to move toward the same level (as they did in Figure 5.1) because of a flow of capital from the S to the K industry.

But investors in industry L (Figure 5.2), will see in KK' (Figure 5.3) an opportunity to increase their earnings, and so funds will flow from

from the influences this chapter discusses. But empirical evidence suggests that even (per-unit) administrative costs fall as the size of the firm increases. See S. Melman, "The Rise of Administrative Overhead in the Manufacturing Industries of the United States 1899–1947," *Oxford Economic Papers*, Vol. III, February 1951, pp. 69–70 and Figs. 4–7.

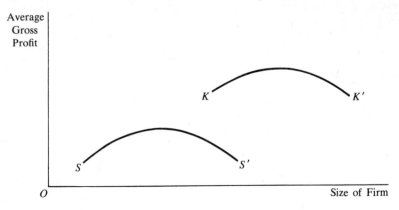

FIG. 5.3

industry *L* to industry *K*. This flow of funds will ordinarily drive *KK'* down somewhat *and will raise LL'*. Thus, so long as any industries are peculiarly well suited to large investments, and so yield disproportionate returns to sizable funds, then, provided capital is prepared to move in response to profit differences, this will tend to be true of all other industries in which large firms operate. No such industry will continue to yield returns as low as those depicted by *LL'* in Figure 5.2, whose peak is no higher than that of *SS'*.

These results can now help us determine the shape of the average gross profits curve (the curve for all industries taken together). Let us

FIG. 5.4

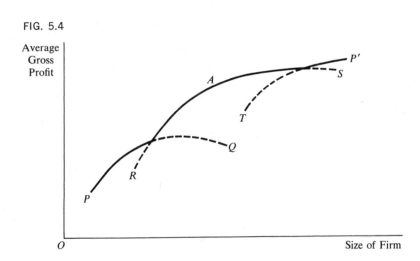

see how this curve is related to the specific investment profit curves (like those shown in the preceding diagrams).

At any level of investment a "rational" entrepreneur will by definition consider investing only in the most profitable of the various opportunities available to him. Thus, the curve of average gross profits, PAP' (Figure 5.4), will be an envelope, that is, it will be the locus at each abscissa, of the highest points on any of the specific investment profit curves (such as PQ, RS, and TP' in Figure 5.4). This means that at every level of investment there is at least one specific investment profit curve tangent to, or coincident with, the average gross profit curve; and that profit maximizing entrepreneurs will invest in no enterprise whose specific investment profit curve is below the average gross profit curve at the point relevant to the quantity of capital they are investing.[5]

We can now argue that (if it is composed of a sufficient number of well-spaced specific investment curves) the average gross profits curve PAP' will be monotonically increasing (its slope will never be negative).[6] This follows directly from the previous argument in which I maintained that there is a tendency for a larger firm to be able to earn at least as much as a smaller firm. That is the significance of LL' being driven to at least equal height with SS' in Figure 5.2. But we also saw that it was implausible that LL' would not be pushed up even further than that diagram shows. If this is so, PAP' will, in fact, have a positive slope. More specifically, the curve will tend to slope upward at least to a point whose abscissa represents so large a volume of money capital that no larger amount can open up more lucrative opportunities *in any industry*, for we have seen that if any industry yields relatively high returns (like those shown by KK' in Figure 5.3) to a large money investment, capital mobility will tend to force up returns for that same volume of investment in all other industries.

[5]I am arguing that average gross profits will be maximized for every given level of investment, i.e., the entrepreneur will invest any quantity of capital in a way that maximizes his profits. This is not equivalent to the assertion (which does not follow from the above) that the entrepreneur will choose the investment level that maximizes his *average* gross profits. The difference is analogous to that between the true assertion that profit maximization requires average costs to be minimized, given the output level, and the generally false statement that output must, for profitability, be set at the point of minimum average costs.

[6]Profit rates may eventually be forced down by rising costs resulting from the presence of scarce resources. The role of scarcity of the management resource has received particular attention in this connection. See N. Kaldor, "The Equilibrium of the Firm," *Economic Journal*, Vol. XLIV, March 1934, and E. A. G. Robinson, *The Structure of Competitive Industry*, New York, Harcourt, Brace & World, 1932, especially Chapter 3.

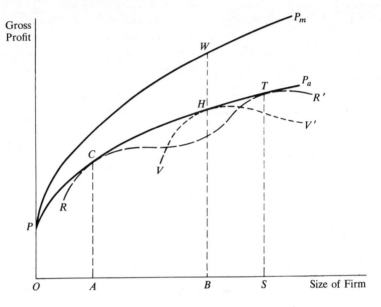

FIG. 5.5

3. Equilibrium of the firm: miscellaneous conclusions

The marginal gross profits curve may readily be derived from this average gross profits curve, and it will, of course, pay an entrepreneur to
invest up to a point where his marginal cost of borrowing is equal to his
marginal gross profit.

Several incidental conclusions may be drawn: The first is that even
if the marginal gross profit is different for every possible size of firm
(as in Figure 5.4), the size of firm may well, but need not, be unique in
any industry;[7] for example, in the situation represented in Figure 5.5,
it will pay to operate in industry V, whose specific investment opportunity profit curve is VV', only if the firm's capital is of magnitude OB.
Thus, if PP_m is the marginal gross profits curve, only an entrepreneur
whose marginal cost of borrowing at scale OB is BW (so that it will in
fact pay him to invest OB) will find it profitable to invest in industry V.
On the other hand, size of firm will not be unique in an industry where
the specific investment profit curve happens to coincide at several

---

[7]Of course, in the case where unlimited funds are available to enterprises there will
be no equilibrium size of firm so long as *marginal* gross profit does not fall. But note
that marginal gross profit may fall even when average gross profit is rising, as in
our diagrams.

points with the curve of average gross profit (for example, RR' in Figure 5.5), and there it will pay for firms of various sizes (OA and OS) to operate simultaneously.

Another conclusion is that it will pay an entrepreneur with relatively limited funds to invest in only one enterprise rather than distribute his funds over several projects, for an entrepreneur who breaks up his investment is faced with the same opportunities as two or more smaller entrepreneurs with combined capital equal to his. If his resources (whatever quantity he happens to use) OS (Figure 5.5) are so divided as to invest OB in one enterprise, and $OA = OS - OB$ in another, then his total profits will be represented by

$$(5.1) \qquad (OA)(AC) + (OB)(BH) \leq (OA + OB)(ST) = (OS)(ST)$$

which is the total profit obtainable by investing all of capital OS in one enterprise. Only in the peculiar case where the average gross profit curve is perfectly horizontal for the stretch CT between A and S need no loss result from splitting up resources; and even in this case the entrepreneur is no better off in consequence of having split his investment but merely loses nothing by it. [8]

A third conclusion follows from the analysis: Suppose an entrepreneur's credit position changes so that he can obtain more (or less) capital than before at every rate of interest. It may be seen that sometimes it will not pay the entrepreneur to expand (or contract) his old enterprise. Instead, it may, in the long run, be more profitable for him to withdraw his capital entirely from the old enterprise and reinvest it in the enterprise which has now become most profitable. Thus, in Figure 5.6, if the entrepreneur's marginal cost of borrowing curve shifts from B_1B_1' to B_2B_2', it will pay him to withdraw his capital from industry J and reinvest in some industry such as K where JJ' and KK' are the specific investment profit curves for industries J and K respectively.

---

[8]Note that a short horizontal stretch in the average gross profit is insufficient to enable entrepreneurs to split up their capital without loss. The curve must be perfectly horizontal at least between the abscissa representing some quantity of capital OS and the abscissa equidistant between S and the origin; for if an entrepreneur splits his capital OS into several parts, at least one of the parts (OA) must be less than or equal to one half of the original capital. If the average gross profits curve is not horizontal for the distance indicated, the average return (AC) on this part (OA) of his investment will be less than the average return (ST) obtainable with capital OS. In this case the "less than or equal to" in (5.1) above should be replaced by "less than," i.e., the splitting up of his capital must necessarily involve a loss for the entrepreneur. This entire argument, of course, abstracts from considerations of risk or peculiarities of taxation arrangements which may increase the desirability of "placing one's eggs in several baskets."

4. Implications for net profit rates

More relevant for our discussion of the motives for accumulation, this analysis may also provide some theoretical basis for Professor Crum's empirical conclusion [9] that, up to a point, rate of profit rises with size of firm. To do this we must assume something about the basic shape of the marginal cost of borrowing curve. We may surmise that an entrepreneur can usually borrow a fairly limited amount without too much difficulty, especially if he has some capital of his own so that he can be said to be borrowing from himself. But the credit of most persons is good only within certain limits and, after those limits are reached, their marginal cost of borrowing rises very sharply, in many cases almost vertically.

FIG. 5.6

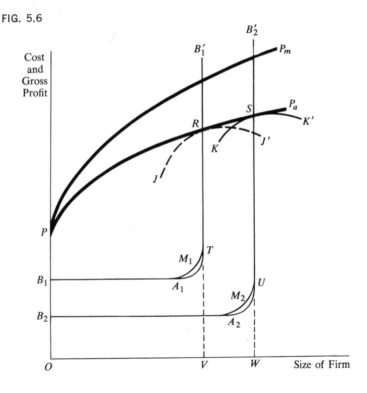

[9] W. L. Crum, *Corporate Size and Earning Power*, Cambridge, Mass., Harvard University Press, 1939. I understand that Professor Crum's computations with more recent data indicate some decline in the rate of profit with size of firm for the largest firms. *Cf.* W. Fellner, *Competition Among the Few*, New York, Knopf, 1949, p. 297, footnote.

In addition, with these marginal cost of borrowing curves and average gross profits curves, *net* profits, like gross profits, will rise with investment if entrepreneurs with better borrowing facilities do not generally pay a much higher rate of interest than do borrrowers with smaller borrowing facilities. I think this is not implausible.

Suppose the curves of marginal and average cost of borrowing for persons with better and poorer credit have the general shape already suggested, that shown in Figure 5.6 by $B_2M_2B_2'$, $B_2A_2B_2'$, $B_1M_1B_1'$, and $B_1A_1B_1'$, respectively. Then, provided OB_1 is no smaller than OB_2, that is, provided the initial cost of borrowing to a person with better credit is no greater than to a person with poorer credit, it is plausible that the rate of interest paid by the former on the money he actually borrows is never higher than that paid by the latter.

The shape of the cost of the borrowing curve—nearly constant at first, and then very sharply rising with almost a right angle at the end of the constant stretch—implies that the first borrower will probably pay a rate of interest slightly higher than OB_1, and the second entrepreneur will probably pay not much more than the rate of interest indicated by OB_2. If PP_m and PP_a are the curves of marginal and average gross profit, then the rates of interest paid by the smaller and larger borrowers will be represented by VT and WU, respectively. The average *gross* profits will be VR and WS, respectively, where WS is no smaller than VR. Because WU is assumed not greater in general than VT, it follows that average *net* profit, here represented by TR for investment OV, and US for investment OW, will tend to rise with the size of the investment.[10]

5. Conclusion

We see then that the businessman's desire to increase his profit lends itself to translation into a desire to expand his firm, for large size may raise the firm's profits more than in proportion to the value of its assets.

[10]It is not my purpose here to go deeper into Professor Crum's methods and conclusions because the analysis neither stands nor falls with them. Two points, however, may be noted: first, while his profits are not computed on a basis directly applicable to my analysis, I have attempted several sample recalculations, none of which shows any significant changes in the results; second, it has been pointed out by Professor Crum, and others, that his smaller firms make smaller profits on the average because so many of them sustain losses. Indeed, profitable small firms appear to have a higher profit rate than do profitable larger firms. However, this need not be inconsistent with my conclusions, because the inferior opportunities left to smaller firms may be inferior mostly because they are riskier, i.e., larger firms may prefer part of their extra profits in the form of insurance. Professor Crum's more recent data suggest, however, that the connection between risk and firm size is not quite so simple. See his *The Age Structure of the Corporate System*, Berkeley, University of California Press, 1953, pp. 93–97.

This, in turn, means that large size can increase the magnitude of the funds he can accumulate to finance further expansion. The businessman must have amassed wealth to be an efficient wealth amasser. These relationships alone can motivate businessmen to work hard to expand the scale of their operations.[11] Later in this book it is shown how this observation can be used as the basis for a model that determines the firm's equilibrium rate of growth.

[11]It is true that it also motivates them to expand by merger but, especially under the operation of the antitrust laws, merger is not always possible. And, in any case, growth by other means is also thereby encouraged.

We may also note, incidentally, that the profit pattern which has been described can make for growing inequality in the size distribution of firms and that the credit market can easily magnify this effect. It has been pointed out that a financial institution determines the amount it is willing to lend to any single borrower, at least in part, by estimating the prospective profitability of the investments for which the money is to be used. (*Cf.*, e.g., F. W. Taussig, *Principles of Economics*, New York, Macmillan, 3rd ed., 1927, p. 352.) But, in many cases, lenders base their estimate of prospective profitability on the profits earned by the borrower in the past. With time, this will only tend to increase the disparity between the amounts of money available to different entrepreneurs, for if my argument is correct, it is the entrepreneur with the greatest capital at his disposal who will have the largest present earnings and who can, therefore, most rapidly augment his funds by borrowing, as well as by accumulation.

CHAPTER 6

The revenue maximization hypothesis

Though businessmen are interested in the scale of their operations partly because they see some connection between scale and profits, I think management's concern with the level of sales goes considerably further. In my dealings with them I have been struck with the importance the oligopolistic enterprises attach to the value of their sales. A small reversal in an upward sales trend that can quite reasonably be dismissed as a random movement sometimes leads to a major review of the concern's selling and production methods, its product lines, and even its internal organizational structure.[1]

Before going on I must make an important terminological point. In ordinary business parlance the term "sales" refers not to the number of physical units of one of its products that has been sold but, rather, to the *total revenue* obtained by the firm from the purchases of its customers. In the near universal multiproduct firm, any measure of over-all physical volume must involve index number problems, and the adoption of a value measure doubtless is to be expected. In any event, in the sequel I shall adhere to the businessman's practice and use the terms "sales" and "total revenue" as synonyms. As a reminder, however, I will frequently employ "dollar sales" or "sales revenue" or some other such expressions.

1. Disadvantages of declining sales

There are many reasons why the businessman should show such concern about the magnitude of his sales. Declining sales can bring with them all sorts of disadvantages: There is reason to fear that consumers will

[1] As has frequently been noted in the empirically based portion of the literature, the oligopolist seems to be equally fearful of any decline in the proportion between his sales and the sales of the rest of the industry. If its market share falls because its rivals are expanding more rapidly, the firm which has not kept up often reacts as though its sales were actually falling. For the moment I shall largely ignore this concern with market share because I deal first with the static theory. However, the point will play a more important role in the dynamic analysis of Part II.

shun a product if they feel it is falling in popularity, though their information on these matters is certainly often spotty. Banks and the money market will tend to be less receptive to the desires of a firm whose absolute or relative sales volume is declining. Perhaps even more important in this connection is the very real danger that firms whose sales are falling will lose distributors—a major marketing setback. Management also is not unmoved by the fact that in a declining firm personnel relations are made much more difficult when firing rather than hiring is the order of the day. The firm that declines (or remains small when others expand) can lose monopoly power and the power to adopt an effective competitive counter strategy when one is called for, and it may become more vulnerable to a general deterioration in business conditions. For all these reasons the executive may reasonably conclude that maintenance of as large a sales volume as possible is the only way to succeed in business.

Even if size did not promote profits, personal self-interest could well induce the managers of a firm to seek to maximize sales. Executive salaries appear to be far more closely correlated with the scale of operations of the firm than with its profitability.[2] And in the modern corporation, which is characterized so often by separation of ownership from management, many executives find it prudent to avoid an absolute or relative decline in their operations. Here, management's concern with the volume of sales is compounded of its very conscientious concern with the responsibilities of its trusteeship and a desire to play good stockholder politics. In any event, the effects are the same—the volume of sales approaches the status of a prime business objective.

2. Sales as an ultimate objective

Up to this point, in essence, I have been arguing that the firm may be expected to promote sales as a means to further its other objectives—operational efficiency and, ultimately, profits. So far, there is no necessary clash with orthodox analysis.

But now I propose to take the next step and suggest that the businessman has gone still further in his regard for sales volume. I believe that to him sales have become an end in and of themselves.

It must be made clear to begin with that this hypothesis in no way conflicts with an assumption of rationality. People's objectives are

[2]A statistical test of this surmise was undertaken by J. W. McGuire, J. S. Y. Chiu, and A. O. Elbing. See their "Executive Incomes, Sales and Profits," *American Economic Review*, Vol. LII, September 1962. Their results do seem to support the view in the text.

whatever they are. Irrationality surely must be defined to consist in decision patterns that make it more difficult to attain one's own ends, and not in choosing ends that, for some reason, are considered to be wrong. Unless we are prepared to determine other people's values, or unless they pursue incompatible objectives, we must class behavior as rational if it efficiently pursues whatever goals happen to have been chosen.

The evidence for my hypothesis that sales volume ranks ahead of profits as the main object of the oligopolist's concern is again highly impressionistic; but I believe it is quite strong. Surely it is common experience that when one asks an executive "How's business?" he will answer that his *sales* have been increasing (or decreasing) and talk about his profit only as an afterthought, if at all. And I am told the requirements for acceptance to membership in the Young Presidents Organization (an honorific society) are that the applicant be under 40 years of age and president of a company whose annual volume is over a million dollars. Presumably it makes no difference if this firm is in imminent danger of bankruptcy.

Nor is this failure to emphasize profits a pure rationalization or a mere matter of careless phrasing. Almost every time I have come across a case of conflict between profits and sales, the businessmen with whom I worked left little doubt as to where their hearts lay. It is not unusual to find a profitable firm in which some segment of its sales can be shown to be highly unprofitable. For example, I have encountered several firms that were losing money on their sales in markets quite distant from the plant, where local competition forced the product price down to a level that did not cover transportation costs. Another case was that of a watch distributor whose sales to small retailers in sparsely settled districts were so few and far between that the salesmen's wages were not made up by the total revenues they brought in. When such a case is pointed out to management, it is usually quite reluctant to abandon its unprofitable markets. Businessmen may consider seriously proposals which promise to put these sales on a profitable basis. There may be some hope for the adoption of a suggestion that a new plant be built nearer the market to which current transportation costs are too high or that watch salesmen be transferred to markets with greater sales potential and a mail order selling system be substituted for direct selling in little populated regions.[3] But a program that explicitly proposes any cut in sales volume, whatever the profit considerations, is likely to meet a cold reception. In many cases firms finally do perform

---

[3]Even this suggestion was not adopted by the watch distibutor.

the radical surgery involved in cutting out an unprofitable line or territory, but this usually occurs after much heart searching and delay.[4]

3. The role of profits

It is tempting to object that along this road lies bankruptcy; and so it would if management were prepared not only to subordinate profit considerations to sales, but to disregard profits altogether. After all, maximum sales might require prices so low that the costs would nowhere be covered.[5] It is quite true that there is some conflict between the firm's sales goal and its profit objectives and, as is to be expected, the matter is settled by compromise. The compromise is, of course, usually tacit, its terms are ill-defined, and doubtless it varies from case to case. But I think it is nevertheless possible to set up a formal relationship which is analytically useful and, at the same time, provides us with a reasonably close approximation to the facts.

The nature of this approximation is again best suggested by an illustrative experience. A manufacturer of a new synthetic yarn indicated that he was reluctant to promote sales by introducing his product at a price that would not cover the cost of his small initial outputs. The firm's usual rate of return on investment played an explicit and very fundamental role in these deliberations. It was made clear that management was not concerned with obtaining profits higher than this. Once this minimum profit level was achieved, sales revenues rather than profits became the overriding objective.

I suspect that the much publicized practice of average cost pricing is a crude attempt to achieve just this sort of goal. Prices are set at a fixed markup above average costs, not only because this is a convenient rule of thumb, but also because the practice appears to set a floor under the rate of return.[6] Of course, it does not always work out in that way

[4]Yet, as will be shown in the next chapter, a good marginalist approach even to *sales* revenue maximization requires abandonment of disproportionately *unprofitable* sales segments. The firm's resources should be allocated among its different products, territories, etc. in such a way that the marginal *profits* from all types of sales are equal. For if the sacrifice of a dollar of profit can produce a greater addition to sales of type A than to sales of type B, then sales cannot be at a maximum (subject to the profit constraint described in the next section of the text) and effort should be transferred from the promotion of B sales to the promotion of sales of A.

[5]But note that maximization of *dollar* sales will never call for zero or negative prices because, at these prices, sales (equal total revenue) must also be zero or negative.

[6]It also helps to prevent profits from going too high and may thereby discourage the entry of new competitors. This consideration explains, in part, the firm's failure to seek to maximize short-run profits. However, I feel that its role in the real firm's calculations has been exaggerated a bit in some of the attempts to rationalize average cost pricing.

because volume can be miscalculated and cost estimates may therefore turn out to be incorrect. But the objective of the procedure seems clear nevertheless.

I am prepared to generalize from these observations and assert that the typical oligopolist's objectives can usefully be characterized, approximately, as sales maximization subject to a minimum profit constraint.[7] Doubtless this premise overspecifies a rather vague set of attitudes, but I believe it is not too far from the truth. So long as profits are high enough to keep stockholders satisfied and contribute adequately to the financing of company growth, management will bend its efforts to the augmentation of sales revenues rather than to further increases in profits.

4. Determination of the minimum profit level

We have yet to discuss how the minimum acceptable profit level is determined. Once we have taken care of this loose end we shall have laid the foundation for a self-contained static oligopoly model, as will be shown in the next chapter. But until something is said about the determination of the minimum profit level the entire analysis is left up in the air. So long as the acceptable profit level is left undetermined, almost any price or output decision is compatible with the stated objectives of the firm.

Once more, almost anything that is said here must be an oversimplification and an overrigid characterization of a fairly amorphous and variable set of business practices. Yet I believe that the following discussion does not represent a very great distortion of the facts.[8]

Like the profit maximizer, the sales maximizing firm must think of tomorrow. Its horizon will normally extend well into the future and, accordingly, it must consider prospective sales along with the sales level it is currently achieving. Then increased future sales also will be encompassed in the basic sales maximization objective.

For its outputs and its sales to grow, the firm will need funds to finance its expansion. These funds can be obtained either internally, out of retained profits, or from external sources—by borrowing or through the issue of new equity. But the availability of external funds

[7]There is nothing new in the observation that firms seek to meet a minimum profit requirement. Thus, e.g., Professor Lintner writes, "The available evidence indicates that many if not most managements do have in mind some sort of minimum return which contemplated investments must satisfy if they are to be undertaken...." (John Lintner, "Effect of Corporate Taxation on Real Investment," *American Economic Review*, Vol. XLIV, May 1954, p. 522.)

[8]The argument which follows is based on a suggestion by Professor Leibenstein, for which I am profoundly grateful.

to the firm will depend also on its earnings.[9] The larger the earnings of the company, the more financing it will be able to obtain from the capital market. The firm will then find it desirable to keep up its profit level as a means of financing future sales—but at the same time, high profits, as we shall see, are likely to require some limitation in its current sales volume. Thus, higher profits promote the firm's goals in one way and conflict with them in another. From this long-run point of view, there is then likely to be some intermediate level of profits that is optimal—one that most effectively serves management's sales maximization objective. Looked at in this way the profit level does not take the form of a constraint. Rather, it becomes an instrument variable whose value is determined as part of the optimality calculation. In Chapter 10, when we get to our company growth models, this will be seen very clearly.

But in the short run the required profit appears to be given exogenously. It does serve as a constraint circumscribing the firm's decisions—one which requires it to provide a rate of return to stockholders sufficient to make certain that the company's securities remain attractive to the capital market.[10]

5. Afterthoughts on sales maximization

Since the publication of the first edition of this book the theoretical literature on managerial motivations has blossomed forth and provided a number of alternative and plausible surmises on the aims of business

[9]In a pure Miller-Modigliani world they may depend only on the firm's earnings and be totally unaffected by their allocation between dividends and retained profits. After all, retained earnings if properly reinvested yield increased future earnings which will bring capital gains to the stockholder. If the firm has made its investment plans independently of its financial decisions (surely optimal investment decisions are not dependent on the sources of the funds used to finance them), then an increase in dividend payments should make absolutely no difference one way or the other to current stockholders. With future plans fixed, the total current value of the firm, V, will also be fixed. Suppose there is a D dollar dividend that is made up for by a D dollar new stock issue. The market value of current stockholders' claims on the firm will have declined from V to $V - D$ which is exactly compensated by their D dollar dividend. See M. H. Miller and F. Modigliani, "Dividend Policy, Growth, and the Valuation of Shares," *Journal of Business*, Vol. XXXIV, October 1961.

[10]This argues, then, that from the point of view of the stockholder, management may be what Simon has called a "satisficer" rather than a maximizer—it may seek merely to provide a return sufficient to keep stockholders contented. Incidentally, because bonds and stocks are substitutes both from the view of the buyer (lender), and from that of the borrower firm that issues them, it may also be argued that, in a rough way, dividends will in the long run also be tied, via the risk premium, to the level of interest rates. Though in the short run there is apparently little correlation between the earnings on stocks and the yields of fixed interest securities, competitive pressures, in the long run, must drive their earnings toward

management. Among these suggestions have been a model in which the size of staff enters the managerial utility function,[11] one in which the firm wishes to maximize profit subject to a constraint on sales,[12] and one in which growth becomes a primary company objective.[13] Of course, the notion that the firm may have objectives other than profits antedates considerably the appearance of this volume.[14] However, the distinguishing characteristic of the more recent writings is the fact that they provide analytical models—that they are operational in the sense that they can yield theorems as interesting as those that can be derived from a profit maximization approach.

I have no basic quarrel with any of these, for it seems to me that any contribution provided by the models of this book consists primarily in the demonstration that alternative assumptions about managerial motivations are tractable analytically. I have never claimed that there is any "correct" model that captures the whole truth about managerial goals in all their subtle shadings and complexity. As a matter of fact, diversity of objectives and variation in motives with the passage of time naturally is to be expected if I am right in my view that it is no more rational for managements to hold one consistent set of goals than it is for them to pursue any other.

It is for this reason that I have been surprised at how consistently the firms with which I have had dealings at least appear to have held to

approximate parity, otherwise the type of security whose yield was consistently lower would eventually run out of takers. If management wishes to maintain dividends and stockholders' capital gains as determined by the course of the price of the company's securities at a level which will be considered adequate, the minimum acceptable rate of profit is then determined by the same apparatus that sets the levels of interest rates. In other words, oligopoly earnings net of risk premium would then approximate the so-called normal rate of profit—that rather mysterious ingredient in the economist's cost calculations.

[11]See O. E. Williamson, *The Economics of Discretionary Behavior*, Englewood Cliffs, Prentice-Hall, 1964, pp. 40ff. See also R. J. Monsen, Jr., and A. Downs, "A Theory of Large Managerial Firms," *The Journal of Political Economy*, Vol. LXXIII, No. 3, June 1965, in which it is assumed that "managers act so as to maximize their own lifetime incomes," p. 225.

[12]See Franklin M. Fisher's review of this book, *Journal of Political Economy*, Vol. LXVIII, June 1960, and D. K. Osborne, "On the Goals of the Firm," *Quarterly Journal of Economics*, Vol. LXXVIII, November 1964.

[13]E.g., Harvey Leibenstein, *Economic Theory and Organizational Analysis*, New York, Harper & Row, 1960, Part IV, and R. Marris, *The Economic Theory of Managerial Capitalism*, Glencoe, The Free Press, 1964, especially Chs. 2 and 3. See also Ch. 10 in this book.

[14]Thus, see the references in Williamson, *op. cit.*, Ch. 2. See also R. F. Lanzillotti, "Pricing Objectives in Large Companies," *American Economic Review*, Vol. XLVIII, December 1958.

some sort of sales and growth objectives. I have come across only one very clear exception, in which the new president of a major company was quoted in the press to the effect that he did not aim to make his firm the largest in the industry—only the most profitable. It is interesting that this man had once been an academic economist.[15]

I will not attempt to reply systematically to criticisms that have been leveled against the sales maximization hypothesis. After all, the question at issue is a factual matter that cannot be settled by *a priori* arguments. Yet it may be useful to comment on a few of these; for example, the suggestion that, for some reason that is to me obscure, companies that pursue this goal are unlikely to survive very long. Indeed, one noted economist caught himself about to argue that a profit maximizing firm would end up outselling its sales maximizing competitor! By definition, the (long-run) sales maximizer must end up the larger while the profit maximizer produces more income for its stockholders, but neither type of firm is an inherently shaky proposition. If long-run sales objectives require larger profits, the rational sales maximizer will do all he can to obtain these profits as an intermediate step toward the achievement of his objective.

Another argument that has been raised against the sales maximization hypothesis asserts that all of the (rather miscellaneous) phenomena that have been used to defend and illustrate it are perfectly consistent with a *long-run* profit maximization goal. That is, the firm may seek to expand its sales today primarily because it considers this to be a good means to earn more money tomorrow. I would still guess that this alternative hypothesis is not generally valid, but I am really somewhat skeptical about the very concept of the long-run goal. It is particularly questionable in a large firm in which there are many centers of power of varying potency and where goals have never been discussed explicitly and formulated (except for purposes of public relations releases, in which the promotion of virtue itself, in effect, is described as the ultimate aim of the corporation). If observed behavior is perfectly consistent either with long-run sales or profit maximization goals, and we are to avoid its attribution to a corporate unconscious that has somehow adopted its goals without their having been revealed to management, must we not simply file suggestions for *long-run* objectives under the heading "not relevant," or at least "not settled"?

[15]Other exceptions may be extremely large firms, such as General Motors, whose managements fear that further expansion will arouse the interest of the trust busters. However, these giants also frequently try to expand by increasing their product lines while holding their market share constant on older products. On the other hand, the mutual life insurance companies, for whom profits are not even readily defined, may be particularly obvious sales maximizers.

CHAPTER 7

A static oligopoly model

The empirical hypothesis of the preceding chapter about the character-istic objectives of modern oligopolistic firms can be used as the basis of a formal analysis that yields several interesting conclusions. Most of this can be accomplished with the aid of fairly simple geometry, but I shall employ some algebra at the end of the chapter in order to gener-alize a few of the propositions. Discussion of the main implications of the analysis has been deferred to later chapters.

1. Price-output determination: partial analysis

It will be remembered that *sales* maximization under a profit constraint does not mean an attempt to obtain the largest possible physical volume (which is hardly easy to define in the modern multiproduct firm). Rather, it refers to maximization of total revenue (dollar sales), which is to the businessman the obvious measure of the amount he has sold.[1] Maximum sales in this sense need not require very large physical out-puts. To take an extreme case, at a zero price physical volume may be high but dollar sales volume will be zero. There normally will be[2] a well-determined output level that maximizes dollar sales. This level ordinarily can be fixed with the aid of the well-known rule: Maximum

[1]We may be tempted to say then that he suffers from money illusion. But this can hardly be taken as a criticism of his rationality—his objectives simply are what they are and there is nothing inherently rational or irrational about them.

[2]Provided there is some price sufficiently high to drive the quantity demanded down to zero, the total revenue function will be bounded from above, i.e., total revenue will be less than or equal to this maximum price multiplied by the quantity which will be demanded when price is zero. The total revenue will be zero both at this maximum demand price and when the price is zero. At intermediate prices it will be positive provided the demand curve has a negative slope throughout. Hence, in such cases at least one maximum total revenue point must exist. If the demand curve is everywhere differentiable such a point will only occur where the price elasticity of demand is unity.

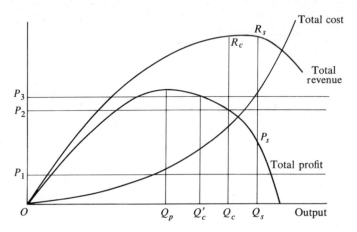

FIG. 7.1

revenue will be attained only at an output at which the elasticity of demand is unity, that is, at which marginal revenue is zero.

But this rule does not take into account the profit constraint. That is, if at the revenue maximizing output the firm does in fact earn enough, or more than enough, profits to meet the competitive requirements, then it will want to produce the sales maximizing quantity. But if at this output profits are too low, the firm's output must be changed to a level that, though it fails to maximize sales, does meet the profit requirement.

We see, then, that two types of equilibria appear to be possible: one in which the profit constraint provides no effective barrier to sales maximization and one in which it does. This is illustrated in Figure 7.1, which shows the firm's total revenue, cost, and profit curves, as indicated. The profit and sales maximizing outputs are, respectively, OQ_p and OQ_s. Now if, for example, the minimum required profit[3] level is OP_1, then the sales maximizing output OQ_s will provide plenty of profit and that is the amount it will pay the sales maximizer to produce. His selling price will then be set at $Q_s R_s/OQ_s$. But if the producer's required profit level is OP_2, output OQ_s, which yields only profit $Q_s P_s$, clearly will not do. Instead, his output will be reduced to level OQ_c, which is just compatible with his profit constraint.

I shall argue presently that, in fact, only equilibrium points in which the constraint is effective (OQ_c rather than OQ_s) can normally be expected to occur when other decisions of the firm are taken into account.

[3]At this point I assume the profit minimum is a fixed total amount. Other possibilities, e.g., a fixed minimum *rate* of return on costs, are considered later.

If, as is normally the case, marginal cost (MC) is positive, the profit maximizing output OQ_p will be no greater (and usually smaller) than the one that yields either type of sales maximum OQ_s or OQ_c. If at the point of maximum profit the firm's marginal costs are positive, an increase in output will increase total sales revenue because marginal revenue must at that point be equal to marginal cost and, hence, it too must be positive. We must have $MR = MC > 0$. Therefore, if at the point of maximum profit the firm earns more profit than the required minimum,[4] it will pay the sales maximizer to lower his price and increase his physical output.

Suppose now that the total profit curve has a single peak, as in Figure 7.1, rather than being composed of several hills and valleys. Then a rise in required minimum profits, if it affects output at all, will cause a rise in price and a decrease in the quantity produced. Starting from a sales maximizing output of either variety, an output level that was just shown to be larger than the profit maximizing quantity, any increase in output will only lower profits. Hence, if the required minimum profit rises, say from OP_2 to OP_3, so that at the initial output OQ_c the profit level is no longer acceptable, the higher required profit level only can be attained by a cut in physical sales (to OQ'_c), that is, by a rise in price.

2. Choice of input and output combinations

The typical oligopolistic firm is a multiproduct enterprise (frequently the number of distinct items runs easily into the hundreds) and, of course, it employs a large variety of inputs. In this section I examine briefly the effect of sales (rather than profit) maximization on the amounts and allocation of the firm's various inputs and outputs.

We obtain the following result, which may at first appear rather surprising: Given the level of expenditure, the sales maximizing firm will produce the same quantity of each output and market it in the same ways as does the profit maximizer. Similarly, given the level of their total revenues, the two types of firm will optimally use the same inputs in identical quantities and will allocate them in exactly the same way. This result may be somewhat implausible because one is tempted to think of some products or some markets as higher profit-lower revenue producers than others, and one would expect the profit maximizing firm to concentrate more on the one variety and the sales maximizing firm to specialize more in the other. But we shall see in a moment why

---

[4] If it earns less than the required minimum at this output, there is obviously no output which will satisfy the profit constraint.

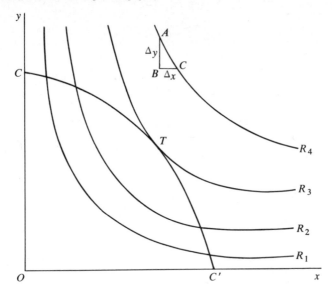

FIG. 7.2

this is not so, though later I shall show that this view contains an element of truth.

It is easy to illustrate our result geometrically. In Figure 7.2 let x and y represent the quantities sold of two different products (or sales of one product in two different markets) or the quantities bought of two different inputs. The curves labeled R_1, R_2, etc. are iso-revenue curves, that is, any such curve is the locus of all combinations of x and y yielding some fixed amount of revenue. Where x and y represent the quantities sold of two products, if their prices were fixed, the R curves would be ordinary (straight) price lines. Their convexity to the origin represents the diminishing marginal revenues from the sale of x and y as their quantities increase, which is the result of their falling prices (negatively sloping demand curves).[5] Similarly, curve CC' represents all combinations of x and y that can be produced with a fixed outlay (total cost). The standard analysis tells us that the point of tangency T,

[5]The absolute value of the slope of such a line equals the ratio of the marginal revenue of x to that of y, for points A and C represent the same total revenue. Hence, the move from A to B represents a loss in revenue ΔR equal to the gain from moving from B to C. That is, we have $\Delta R = \Delta y \cdot MR_y = MR_x \cdot \Delta x$ (approximately), so that $\Delta y/\Delta x = MR_x/MR_y$. Therefore, the falling slope of an R curve as x increases implies a falling marginal revenue of x relative to that of y. Even if the demand curves for x and y are linear the iso-revenue curves will be nonlinear (quadratic). If the demand equations are $P_x = a_x - b_x x$ and $P_y = a_y - b_y y$ then the iso-revenue equations will be $K = P_x x + P_y y = a_x x - b_x x^2 + a_y y - b_y y^2$. A similar discussion applies to the input analysis.

between CC' and one of the R curves, is the point of profit maximization. But it is also the point of revenue maximization because it lies on the highest revenue curve attainable with this outlay. This demonstrates our result.

A little reflection should now render the result quite plausible. The point is simply that, *given the level of costs*, because profit equals revenue minus costs, whatever maximizes profits must maximize revenues. Hence, differences between the profit and the sales maximizer's output composition or resource allocation must be attributed not to a reallocation of a given level of costs (or revenues), but to the larger outputs (and, therefore, total costs and revenues) that, we have seen, are to be expected to accompany sales maximization.[6]

Explained in the way we have just done, our theorem is completely trivial. But when the sales maximizer's profit constraint is taken into account, a more interesting but closely related conclusion can be drawn.

We may view the difference between maximum attainable profits and the minimum profit level expected by the sales maximizer as a fund of sacrificeable profits which is to be devoted to increasing revenues as much as possible.[7] Because each output is produced beyond the point of maximum profits its marginal profit yield will, of course, be negative. In other words, each time it increases the output of some product in order to increase its total revenue the firm must use up more of its fund of sacrificeable profits. This fund of sacrificeable profits must be allocated among the different outputs, markets, inputs, etc. in a way which maximizes total dollar sales. The usual reasoning indicates that this requires the marginal revenue yield of a dollar of profit sacrificed, for example, by product x, to be the same as that obtained from a dollar of profit lost to any other product y. In other words, we must have

$$\frac{\text{marginal revenue product of } x}{\text{marginal profit yield of } x} = \frac{\text{marginal revenue product of } y}{\text{marginal profit yield of } y}.$$

[6]We conclude that when the operations researcher encounters the problem of allocating optimally some *fixed* quantity of a firm's resources, as when a division of a firm or a government agency has a fixed budget allocated to it, the values of all other decision variables being given, his answer will be exactly the same, whether he is dealing with a sales or a profit maximizing firm.

[7]Provided, of course, that sales maximization does not permit a surplus of profits over the required minimum, as would be the case (Fig. 7.1) when required minimum profit is OP_1 so that the sales maximizing output OQ_s is optimal. But as already noted, I shall argue in a later section that this will not normally occur, i.e., that the profit constraint ordinarily will be effective.

This relationship indicates that, even in the sales maximizing firm, relatively unprofitable inputs and outputs are to be avoided, whatever the level of outlay and total revenue.

3. Advertising and service competition

As Professors Chamberlin and Brems have emphasized, firms characteristically compete not only in terms of price; in fact, more typically the oligopolist's competitive strategy is planned in terms of advertising outlay, product modification, and special services offered the buyer. The decision as to how far to carry each of these activities can be influenced profoundly by the firm's choice of objectives—whether it chooses to maximize sales or profits.

I shall discuss explicitly only the decision on the magnitude of the advertising budget because it is so easily quantifiable. However, the analogy with service and product characteristic planning is fairly clear and certainly suggestive.

The relevant diagram for the advertising decision is completely elementary. On the horizontal axis in Figure 7.3 I represent the magnitude of advertising expenditure, and on the vertical axis, total sales (revenue) and total profit. In drawing the total revenue curve I assume, as most businessmen seem to, that increased advertising expenditure can always increase physical volume, though, after a point, sharply diminishing returns may be expected to set in.[8] This means that total revenue must vary with advertising expenditure in precisely the same manner. Unlike a price reduction, a *ceteris paribus* rise in advertising expenditure involves no change in the market value of the items sold. Hence, while an increase in physical volume produced by a price reduction may or may not increase dollar sales, depending on whether demand is elastic or inelastic, an increase in volume brought about by added advertising outlay must always be accompanied by a proportionate increase in total revenue.

The 45° line, as usual, is able to transfer data on advertising expenditure from the horizontal to the vertical axis, that is, advertising outlay OA is equal to AK. The other costs of the firm (OC) are taken to be

[8]Of course, this is not necessarily true—potential customers may perhaps be repelled by excessive advertising.

This diagram, incidentally, assumes implicitly that the price already has somehow been determined. Of course, in a more general analysis, such as that provided in the mathematical notes at the end of this chapter, prices and advertising outlays will be determined simultaneously. For a good geometric treatment of the interdependence of price and advertising decisions, see R. L. Sandmeyer, "Baumol's Sales-Maximization Model: Comment," *American Economic Review*, Vol. LIV, December 1964.

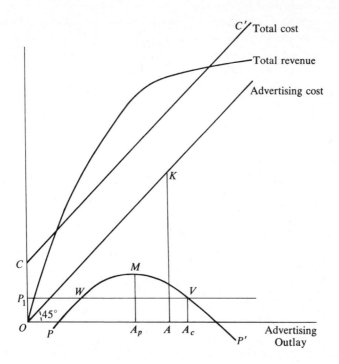

FIG. 7.3

independent of the level of advertisement, because it simplifies but does not invalidate the argument.[9] If these other costs are added (vertically) to the advertising cost curve (45° line), we obtain the line CC', which depicts the firm's total (production, distribution, and selling) costs as a function of advertising outlay. Finally, subtracting these total costs from the level of dollar sales at each level of advertising outlay, we obtain a total profits curve PP'.

We see that the profit maximizing expenditure is OA_p, at which PP' attains its maximum M. If, on the other hand, the sales maximizer's minimum acceptable profit level is OP_1, the constrained sales maximizing advertising budget level is OA_c. It is to be noted that there is no possibility of an unconstrained sales maximum that is analogous to

[9]In fact, this assumption is virtually certain to be false, for if advertising increases physical sales volume it must surely increase total production and distribution costs. We may prefer to interpret the diagram as a cross section of three-dimensional revenue and cost functions taken perpendicular to the output axis, so that advertising is permitted to increase total revenue only by allowing a rise in the price at which the given output is sold.

output OQ_s in Figure 7.1. By assumption, unlike a price reduction, increased advertising always increases total revenue. As a result, it will always pay the sales maximizer to increase his advertising outlay until he is stopped by the profit constraint—until profits have been reduced to the minimum acceptable level. This means that sales maximizers will normally advertise no less than, and usually more than, profit maximizers. Unless the maximum profit level A_pM is no greater than the required minimum OP_1, it will be possible to increase advertising somewhat beyond the profit maximizing level OA_p without violating the profit constraint. Moreover, this increase will be desired because, by assumption, it will increase physical sales, and with them, dollar sales will rise at least proportionately.[10]

4. Determination of prices and outputs: multivariable analysis

The interrelationship between output and advertising decisions now permits us to see the reason for my earlier assertion that an unconstrained sales maximizing output OQ_s (Figure 7.1) will ordinarily not occur. If price is set at a level that yields such an output, profits will be above their minimum level and it will pay to increase sales by raising expenditure on advertising, service, or product specifications. This is an immediate implication of the theorem that there will ordinarily be no unconstrained sales maximizing advertising level. Because its marginal revenue is always positive, advertising can always be used to increase sales to a point where profits are driven to their minimum admissible level.

In fact, we can strengthen this result and rule out even the possibility that, by coincidence, the profit constraint will happen to be satisfied exactly at the point of maximum revenue OQ_s so that this point will coincide with OQ_c. At the point of maximum total revenue, the marginal revenue of each output must be zero. On the other hand, the

[10]In one very large corporation for which I have worked, profit constraint plays a perfectly explicit role in advertising decisions. Profit goals are set by top management and divisions are under strong pressure to meet them. If at the end of the fiscal year a division expects to fall short of its profit target, it cuts advertising outlays drastically. Moreover, if the division seems likely to exceed its profit norm, sharp rises in advertising are rapidly arranged. The advertising agencies have apparently resigned themselves to the added uncertainty to which this very radical short-run profit constraint subjects them. It has been suggested that for a division manager the profit constraint may serve in this way as an efficient profit storage device whereby he may put aside excessive current profits against a future rainy day. By advertising more out of high profits this year he may reap the fruits next year. Company practice usually does not permit direct storage of division profits for the future, so such a device may be very welcome to the division management.

marginal revenue of advertising expenditure is presumably positive. Hence, the equilibrium condition (analogous with that of Section 2, above)

$$\frac{\text{marginal revenue of product } x}{\text{marginal profit yield of product } x} = \frac{\text{marginal revenue of advertising}}{\text{marginal profit yield (cost) of advertising}}$$

can never be satisfied at such a point because the *marginal* profit yield of (or loss from) advertising is always finite.

Examining further the multivariable (many products, many types of advertising expenditure) case, we shall see that some over-all validity remains to two basic results of the earlier part of this chapter: that the sales maximizing outputs will exceed those which maximize profits and that a reduction in the minimum acceptable profit level will increase both outputs and advertising expenditures. However, these conclusions do require some modification in detail—for there may be some exceptional products or types of advertising expenditure for which they do not hold.

First, to see the sense in which the results retain their over-all validity, we note that as the profit requirement is reduced, production, distribution, and selling expenditure must be increased in total, so that at least some outputs or some types of advertising activity must have risen. The reason these costs must grow is almost a matter of arithmetic—as the profit constraint is weakened, total revenue is permitted to increase. But, if revenue grows and profits fall, it follows by subtraction that total costs must become larger.[11]

While there is necessarily an inverse relationship between the minimum profit requirement and the over-all levels of output and advertising, this need not be true of every type of product and promotion outlay, for it is possible that there will be some commodities that are

[11]In particular, we can conclude that there will be an over-all growth in output and advertising in a move from profit to (unconstrained) sales maximization, for profit maximization is equivalent to constrained sales maximization where nothing less than maximum profit is acceptable, while pure sales maximization is tantamount to an appropriately low (possibly negative) profit requirement. Of course, there may be no finite amount of advertisement which yields (unconstrained) maximum sales, although here we must probably give up our assumption that advertisement always yields positive marginal revenues. A simple alternative form of the argument employs the notation $P_{\max} = R_p - C_p$ for the profit maximizer's total profits, revenues, and costs and $P_s = R_{\max} - C_s$ for those of the sales maximizer. Because $P_{\max} > P_s$ and $R_{\max} > R_p$, then $C_s = R_{\max} - P_s > R_p - P_{\max} = C_p$, so that the sales maximizer's production and advertising outlays will never fall short of those of the profit maximizer.

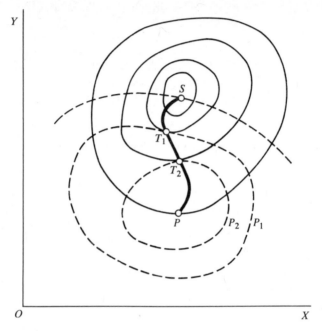

FIG. 7.4

fairly profitable but are inferior revenue producers. These play a role completely analogous with that of inferior goods in the theory of consumer behavior. When revenues and over-all outputs are reduced by stricter profit requirements, these inferior outputs and, perhaps, the funds to be spent advertising them will rise.

This is illustrated in Figure 7.4. Here point S represents the dollar sales maximizing combination of outputs x and y, and the profit maximizing combination is represented by point P. The solid contour lines surrounding point S are iso-total revenue curves—that is, any such curve is the locus of points representing all output combinations yielding equal total revenue. These are closed curves because too high an output can reduce total revenues just as much as can one that is too low.[12] Similarly, the broken curves are iso-profit loci.

When the minimum acceptable profit level corresponds to curve P_1, the highest total revenue that can be attained (the iso-revenue curve closest to point S) is that which is tangent with iso-profit curve P_1.

[12]It may be illuminating to think of these as contour lines for a three-dimensional total revenue hill whose peak is at S.

The point of tangency T_1 is clearly the optimal output combination. Now, suppose the required profit level is increased to that which corresponds to P_2 (P_2 involves higher profits than P_1 because it is closer to P). The equilibrium point will then move to T_2. But in the situation shown in the diagram T_2 is below and to the right of T_1—that is, the increased profit requirement has reduced the output of y and increased the output of x. Thus, because of this perverse behavior, x is classified as an inferior output.

Note, finally, that the dark line PS is the locus of all the points of tangency such as T_1 and T_2. This curve must go through the profit maximizing point P, as the geometry of the diagram clearly shows. Economically, this is tantamount to the assertion, which has already been made, that the profit maximizing output (which yields profits P^*) is obviously also the output that maximizes sales under the constraint that profit must not fall short of P^*. Because all constrained sales maximization points are points of tangency between an iso-revenue and an iso-profit curve, the same must be true (in a limiting sense) of point P. For similar reasons point S will also lie on the line connecting these points of tangency.[13]

5. Relationship to "full cost" pricing

The results of the analysis may suggest that revenue maximization differs very little from average cost pricing. In the single product, single decision variable firm the profit constrained sales maximizer sets a price that yields its average costs plus the minimum acceptable profit. This is seen more clearly with the aid of Figure 7.5, which represents a situation like that shown in Figure 7.1 but in which the vertical axis now measures average, rather than total revenues, costs, and profits. The average cost and average revenue curves are of the usual variety and require no explanation. The minimum per unit profit curve is a rectangular hyperbola representing all combinations of quantity and unit profits that

[13]Locus PS is a sort of contract curve. From any point such as T_1 on the curve it is impossible to increase sales without decreasing profits or to increase profits without cutting into sales, while from any point off PS it is possible to increase both profits and sales. Both the point representing maximal sales subject to a profit constraint and the point of maximum profits under a sales constraint must lie on PS. Hence, the formal resemblance between the requirements of the two models noted in D. K. Osborne, "On the Goals of the Firm," *Quarterly Journal of Economics*, Vol. LXXVIII, November 1964, and the comment by Franklin M. Fisher, *op. cit.*, Vol. LXXIX, August 1965. *Cf.* also M. Hall, "On the Goals of the Firm: Comment," *op. cit.*, Vol. LXXX, February 1966.

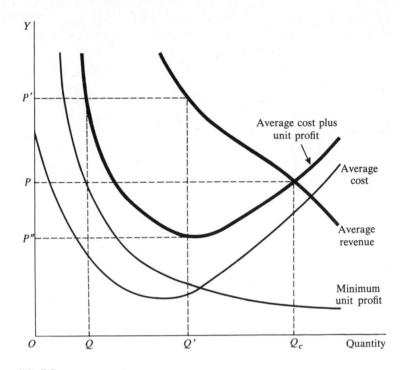

FIG. 7.5

yield the minimum acceptable total profit P_m. This curve is given by the equation $P_m = Q \cdot T$, where Q is the quantity sold and T is profit per unit sold.

If we add the minimum unit profit curve vertically to the average cost curve, we obtain a curve that shows for each output the price that must be charged in order to cover costs plus the required profits. At output OQ_c this curve cuts the average revenue curve, and this is our equilibrium output OQ_c of Figure 7.1.

The resemblance to full cost pricing is undeniable. But I shall show now that the theory of profit constrained sales maximization, far from being an elaborate superstructure imposed on full cost pricing, differs very considerably from the other.[14] The first difference lies in the theoretical analysis of the minimum acceptable profit level: full costing discussions have justly been criticized for leaving unexplained the level

[14] There is some relationship, however, and I believe that average cost pricing can usefully be interpreted as a rule-of-thumb approximation to sales maximization, as was suggested in the preceding chapter.

of "normal" profit. So long as no one profit level is specified, any price-output combination is compatible with average cost pricing, and that hypothesis can explain very little. However, this is not a structural difference between the two hypotheses under discussion.[15] The failure to fix the profit level can easily be remedied by incorporating into full costing discussions the analysis of profit level determination in Chapter 10 or some substitute.

A more fundamental difference between the two pricing hypotheses lies in the marginalist calculations implicit in sales maximization (or in the maximization or minimization of any other variable, for that matter). This difference becomes important when, as is always the case in practice, the firm has more than one decision variable (several product

[15]Sales maximization also differs from full costing in that it is not associated with an assumption of constant average prime costs. This too may be considered a non-structural difference. Even with this premise, it is not clear how the average coster ends up with a price at which the quantity demanded is such as to make his average cost differ from his profits by the amount of his required unit profit. For example, if as the result of a market survey a businessman expects to sell OQ (Figure 7.5), his full cost price will be OP'. But at that price he will actually find he can sell OQ' and earn more profit than he expected because, even if his prime costs are constant, his *unit* fixed costs will have fallen as a result of the rise in his volume. Presumably he must then be taken to lower his price accordingly (in the first instance to OP'') and, hence, to approach the equilibrium full cost price OP in a sequence of steps.

Unfortunately, we cannot depend on such a sequence of prices to approach the equilibrium full-cost price. In fact, in the not implausible case where the curve of unit cost plus required profits has a slope steeper than that of the average revenue (demand) curve, the sequence of full cost prices will move further and further from the equilibrium point. This case was eloquently described by Cassel: "Let us suppose that a travel agency has ordered special trains for a number of Sundays and has contracted to pay 250 *mark* for each train. Each train was to provide 400 seats, all third class. The first Sunday the agency charged 2 *mark* and 125 excursionists bought tickets. The gross receipts amounted to 250 *mark* or to exactly as much as the outlays. The managers of the agency then said to themselves: 'at this price we can only just cover our own costs, but we must also earn something,' and they raised the fare to 3 *mark*. On the next Sunday only 50 people bought tickets. The result was takings of 150 *mark* and a net loss of 100 *mark*. The agency then reasoned: 'average costs amount to 5 *mark* per person and we carry each passenger for 3 *mark;* we cannot go on like this.' The price was raised to 6 *mark* with the result that on the next Sunday the train carried only 6 passengers. The loss rose to 214 *mark*." Gustav Cassel, "The Principles of Railway Rates for Passengers," *International Economic Papers*, No. 6 (translated from *Archiv für Eisenbahnwesen*, 1900), p. 133. This passage was called to my attention by Professor Schneider. Cassel, incidentally, concludes his story charmingly: "Now at last the managers of the agency said to themselves: 'this story of costs must be sheer nonsense, for it only ends in losses.' So they reduced the price straight away to 1 *mark*. The result was brilliant: 400 passengers turned up the next Sunday, a profit of 150 *mark* was earned and, strangest of all, costs had fallen to 0.625 *mark* per head."

prices or one price and the accompanying advertising outlay, etc.[16]).
For example, if there are two or more outputs, sales maximization will
ordinarily involve most of them *not* earning the unit profit called for by
the constraint. Some products will earn unit profits higher than this,
and the unit profits of the others will be sufficiently below the required
level for earnings to average out correctly. The equalities that follow
from sales maximization are all marginal. They assert, as we have
already seen, that the *marginal* profitabilities of any two activities must
be proportional to their *marginal* revenues. This yields no simple
pricing rule and certainly no average cost pricing rule. We must conclude that in the multiproduct or, at least, multiple activity firms that
constitute the economy's business enterprises, sales maximization
cannot be presumed to yield a full cost price on *any* commodity, or a
"normal" profit to *any* activity.

6. The form of the profit constraint

Except for the preceding section, throughout this chapter I have
assumed for geometric simplicity that the minimum profit requirement
refers to the level of *total* profits and states, for example, that the firm
must earn at least $2 million in profits next year. Of course, in practice,
few businessmen have such explicit and clear-cut profit goals. And it
may be expected that in many cases the firm's minimum profit goal will
be approximated better by the requirement that it earns at least, say,
8 percent on its investment or 20 percent on its costs or 15 percent on its
dollar sales. Certainly the argument of the previous chapter, that the
acceptable minimum profit is set, roughly, by competitive conditions to
maintain the attractiveness of the company's securities, suggests that
we must be dealing with a minimum rate of return on investment. It is
not difficult to amend the preceding geometric analysis to accord with
any of these alternatives by taking the required profit level to be shown
by a nonhorizontal line, unlike those in Figures 7.1 and 7.3. For
example, if required minimum profits are fixed as some proportion of
total costs, the minimum profit line in Figure 7.1 will rise with the level
of output in proportion with the height of the total cost curve. It is

---

[16]The reason no difference arises in the one variable case is that the value of this
one variable is determined by the profit constraint, and so there is nothing, or
practically nothing, to maximize. The "practically" refers to the fact that several
values of the variable may satisfy the profit constraint (points W and V in Fig. 7.3),
and sales maximization is then able to choose among them (point V). More generally,
the profit constraint (ignoring the uniqueness problem) will reduce the number of
degrees of freedom to one less than the number of variables whose values can
independently be chosen by the firm.

easily seen that none of the previous analysis and its conclusions is affected. This costless generalization and the generalization to n commodities can also be achieved with the aid of "a little potted calculus," as will now be shown.[17]

MATHEMATICAL NOTES[18]

a. *Generalization of the profit constraint*

It is convenient for our purposes to shortcut the usual analysis of the equilibrium of the firm by assuming that we have already determined what is its cost function $C(X_1, X_2, \ldots, X_n)$ where X_i is the firm's output of commodity i. Let $P_1, P_2, \ldots, P_n$ represent the prices of the various commodities produced by the firm, and let $A_1, A_2, \ldots, A_m$ represent the amounts of the different types of advertising expenditure open to the firm. For economy of notation, I write R for $\Sigma P_i X_i$ to represent the total revenue of the firm, and A for the sum of its advertising costs ΣA_k.

The minimum *total* profit constraint condition of the sort employed earlier in this chapter can be written

$$(7.1) \qquad R - C - A \geq K_1.$$

If, instead, profits are required to equal or exceed some fixed *proportion* of costs, we have

$$\frac{R - C - A}{C + A} \geq K_2$$

or

$$R - (1 + K_2)(C + A) \geq 0.$$

Similarly, if profits are to be, at least, some minimum proportion of dollar sales, we require

$$\frac{R - C - A}{R} \geq K_3$$

or, because K_3 is presumably less than unity,

$$R - \frac{C + A}{1 - K_3} \geq 0.$$

[17]The reader may be interested in comparing the material of this chapter with that of Professor Schneider, which is in a similar spirit and is based on a somewhat similar empirical foundation. See E. Schneider, "Der Realismus der Marginalanalyse in der Preistheorie," *Weltwirtschaftliches Archiv*, Band 73, 1954.

[18]The reader may wish to see the extensions of the following discussion in the interesting comparative statics analysis provided by O. E. Williamson; see his *The Economics of Discretionary Behavior*, Englewood Cliffs, Prentice-Hall, 1964, Chs. 4 and 5.

Finally, if we require profits not to fall short of some minimum proportion of the firm's total investment, and take investment to be a linear function, $I + k_c C + k_a A$, of the two types of cost, we have

$$\frac{R - C - A}{I + k_c C + k_a A} \geq K_4$$

or

$$R - (1 + K_4 k_c)C - (1 + K_4 k_a)A \geq K_4 I.$$

It will be noted that all four of these constraints are special cases of the more general constraint

(7.2) $R - VC - WA \geq K$

where V, W, and K are constants, the first two of which may be assumed to be positive while K may be taken to be nonnegative.

b. *Profit level and the composition of output*

We may formalize the sales maximizer's problem to be maximization of total revenue R, subject to the generalized inequality constraint (7.2.) Because the values of all the variables are to be nonnegative, this is clearly a programming problem. But for our purposes it is more convenient to deal with the corresponding constrained maximum problem using the tools of the differential calculus. Fortunately, this can be done, because we know that the constraint will always be effective (for a rigorous argument see below). Thus, using the Lagrange multiplier, λ, we obtain by partial differentiation of the Lagrangian expression for maximization of R subject to (7.2):

(7.3) $Rx_i - \lambda(Rx_i - VCx_i) = 0 \qquad i = 1, 2, \ldots, n$

and

(7.4) $Ra_k - \lambda(Ra_k - W) = 0 \qquad k = 1, 2, \ldots, m$

where we use the symbol Rx_i to represent the partial derivative of R with respect to X_i, etc.

Let us now rewrite (7.3) as

(7.5) $(1 - \lambda)Rx_i = -\lambda VCx_i$

and divide this equation for commodity i by the corresponding commodity j relationship. This yields

$$\frac{Rx_i}{Rx_j} = \frac{Cx_i}{Cx_j}$$

which states simply that the ratio of the marginal revenues of the two commodities must equal the ratio of their marginal costs. Thus, we see that this rule of profit maximization holds also under sales maximization. A similar result obviously can be obtained for the relationship between two types of advertising expenditure.

Equation (7.3) can also be given another interpretation. Going back to the original forms of the profit constraints, we note that in each case the left-hand side can be described as the profit measure the firm considers significant. We may then, instead of the generalized profit constraint (7.2), employ the equivalent requirement

significant profit level $\geq k_0$.

Our problem is to maximize total revenue subject to the equality form of this last constraint. The Lagrangian expression that corresponds to (7.3) becomes

$$\frac{\partial \text{ total revenue}}{\partial X_i} - \lambda \frac{\partial \text{ significant profit level}}{\partial X_i} = 0.$$

Subtracting the second term from both sides and dividing by the same equation for commodity j we have

$$\frac{\text{marginal revenue of } i}{\text{marginal revenue of } j} = \frac{\text{marginal profit loss (or gain) from } i}{\text{marginal profit loss (or gain) from } j}$$

a condition that was referred to earlier in this chapter.

c. Justification of the equality form of the constraint

I now prove that on the usual economic assumptions constraint (7.2) can never turn out to be a strict inequality at the optimal point. To show this, I prove that when (7.2) holds as an equation, marginal revenue must be positive so that the unconstrained revenue maximum (assuming it is unique) must require larger outputs than are permitted by the constraint.

Proof: From (7.5) we note that marginal revenue is given by

$$(7.6) \qquad Rx_i = -\frac{\lambda}{1 - \lambda} VCx_i.$$

Because V and marginal cost Cx_i are both positive, we need merely show that this is also true of the fraction $-\lambda/1 - \lambda$. By (7.4) we have

$$\frac{Ra_k}{W} = -\frac{\lambda}{1 - \lambda}.$$

Here W is positive, as noted above [see (7.2)]. Moreover, the numerator of the left-hand side, the marginal revenue of advertising, has been assumed to be positive (though of course this revenue need not be sufficient to cover the marginal cost of the advertisements). Therefore, $-\lambda/1 - \lambda$ must be positive as well. It follows by (7.6) that the marginal revenue of i must be positive when dollar sales are maximized under the equality form of constraint (7.2) (QED).

d. *Remark on profit maximization and (unconstrained)*
   sales maximization

It is very easy to show that, on our assumptions, the profit and the sales maximizing points will normally not coincide. Pure profit maximization requires (differentiating $R - C - A$ partially with respect to the X's and the A's)

$$Rx_i - Cx_i = 0 \qquad i = 1, \ldots, n$$
$$Ra_k - 1 = 0 \qquad k = 1, \ldots, m.$$

Similarly, pure sales maximization requires

$$Rx_i = 0 \quad \text{and} \quad Ra_k = 0.$$

Hence, if the Rx_i and Ra_k are single valued functions of the X's and the A's, the two sets of equations cannot have the same solutions, and they must both usually differ from those of the *constrained* sales maximization equations (7.3) and (7.4).

CHAPTER 8

Some implications of the oligopoly model

The analysis of the preceding chapter has a number of implications for various areas in economic theory, most of which I did not foresee when I first began to work with the sales maximization hypothesis. First, I shall argue that it can be used to explain some types of business behavior that often have been observed in practice but are difficult to rationalize in terms of a profit maximization objective.

1. Pricing and changes in overhead costs

Students consistently find one of the most surprising conclusions of the theory of the firm to be the assertion that overhead costs do not matter. So long as these costs really do not vary with the level of output, and provided that it does not lead the firm to close down altogether, no change in the level of its overhead costs should lead the profit maximizing firm to change either its prices or its outputs. This piece of received doctrine is certainly at variance with business practice, where an increase in fixed costs[1] is usually the occasion for serious consideration of a price increase.

It is easy to show, however, that this is precisely the sort of response one would expect of the firm that seeks to maximize sales and treats its profits as a constraint, rather than as an ultimate objective. For if, in equilibrium, the firm always earns only enough to satisfy its profit constraint, as I argued in the previous chapter, then a rise in overhead cost must mean that earnings fall below the acceptable minimum if no compensating changes are made. The result is precisely the same as that of an increase in the minimum profit level; outputs and/or advertising expenditures must be reduced in order to make up the required profits.

[1] I use the terms "fixed costs" and "overheads" loosely, treating them as synonyms, although this is not standard practice.

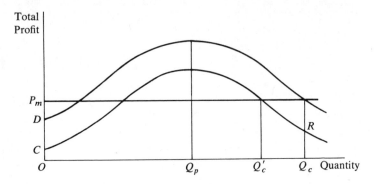

FIG. 8.1

The purpose of any such decrease in production is, of course, to permit an increase in selling price.

This is very easily restated in terms of Figure 8.1. An increase in overhead costs means, geometrically, a uniform downward shift in the total profit curve by the amount of the overhead expenses. Hence, if overheads rise by amount CD, output will fall from OQ_c to OQ'_c, for at OQ_c profits will now be Q_cR, which is less than the minimum acceptable level, OP_m. By contrast, the change in overhead costs will leave the profit maximizing output unchanged at OQ_p.

Again, inferior outputs and types of advertising constitute an exception. Sales of these relatively ineffective revenue earners will be increased when increased overheads force the firm to husband its profits more carefully. However, I doubt whether this exception is likely to be very important. Certainly, one would not expect it to loom large in the actual behavior of business firms whose rough and ready decision-making processes are likely to bypass the more subtle adjustments called for by optimization analysis.

In line with this last remark, I do not wish to go too far in rationalizing the businessman's behavior with respect to overhead costs. It is plausible that prices are sometimes raised in response to an increase in fixed cost simply because executives are making their pricing decisions in accord with a crude average cost pricing rule of thumb—if costs rise, so must prices. And there is little doubt that average cost pricing is sometimes misused to serve the businessman's interests badly. High prices are charged because costs are high at current low output levels—without consideration of the possibility that lower prices can increase volume and so may reduce unit costs. I have come across several such cases. But we must be careful not to sell the businessman short—he is often shrewd and well educated by experience. I believe that it is not much of an exaggeration to say that the constrained sales maximum hypothesis often is a fairly close approximation to the rationale of the business-man's response to changes in his fixed costs.

2. Nonprice competition

Economists have often noted the oligopolist's reluctance to employ price cutting as a competitive weapon. But this cannot be explained entirely as a manifestation of a desire to live the quiet life, for even when competitive activity does become more vigorous it is notorious that this is very likely to take the form of more advertising expenditure or the introduction of new product features, some of which are sometimes considered to be little more than frills. It would appear then that the large firm's competitive effort has been channeled away from price policy and into advertising, service, and product characteristic modification.

This phenomenon is not a necessary consequence of sales maximiza-tion any more than of profit maximization. But the sales maximization hypothesis can certainly help to account for the psychology behind these practices.

To see why this is so, we must remember that to the businessman "sales" mean total revenue, not physical volume. Now, a dollar spent on advertising, if it increases physical volume, must necessarily increase total revenue. But a price reduction is a double-edged sword which, while it serves as an influence to increase total revenue in that it usually adds to the number of units that can be sold, it simultaneously works in the opposite direction by reducing the revenue on each unit sold. In other words, as the economist knows so well, price cutting is an uncertain means for increasing dollar sales because its success depends on the elasticity of demand.

True, price cutting is equally undependable as a method of increasing profits—indeed more so, for if it fails to increase total revenue, it must almost certainly reduce profits—because the resulting increase in out-puts must also add to total costs. But, on the other hand, the direction of the effect of advertising, improved service, etc., on sales is fairly certain while, very often, their profitability may be quite doubtful. Thus, sales maximization makes far greater the presumption that the business-man will consider *non*price competition to be the more advantageous alternative.

3. Implications for ideal output analysis

Because of the theorist's failure to formulate a well-defined theory of oligopoly pricing (even the kinked demand curve analysis indicates why price may tend to stay where it is and not where it was set in the first place), oligopolistic output has never been subjected to much explicit analysis by welfare economists in their discussions of ideal output. One comes away only with a rather vague general feeling that after all the oligopolist is practically a monopolist, and so he is very likely to fall under the same cloud as an output restrictor. One suspects that his outputs are smaller than they would be under the full reign of consumer (or rather, public) sovereignty.

The sales maximization hypothesis does provide us with an analysis of oligopolistic pricing and output determination. Unfortunately, it does not seem to open the way to firm and simple welfare judgments (though what market form *can* be evaluated categorically?). However, some impressionistic conclusions can be drawn.

We first recall that under sales maximization, outputs will tend to be larger, over-all, than they would be under profit maximization. However, they may be smaller than those that would result in zero profits, that is, smaller than the output levels that are often misleadingly called competitive.[2] This means that in a world in which competition was perfect everywhere else, the allocation of resources to an oligopolistic industry would perhaps be too small—though less so than one would be led to expect by a profit maximization hypothesis.

But approximations to perfect competition are rare, and marginal cost pricing, if it is to be found at all, is the exception rather than the rule, even in governmentally operated enterprises. Even this weak condemnation of the oligopolistic resource allocation, therefore, must be considered suspect. Because other industries also fail to bid for resources with energy as great as that which is to be expected of perfect competition, there is no reason to feel that the oligopolistic firm gets less than its appropriate share. Indeed, if it is true that competition sets the level of the minimum profit rate so that in all firms costs bear a somewhat similar relation to prices, we may surmise that some sort of rough parity is established and that oligopolistic pricing leads to an allocation of resources as close to the optimum as can reasonably be expected.[3] That is, the distortions may tend roughly to cancel out.

[2]But if, as mentioned in Ch. 6, the minimum acceptable profit level tends in the long run to approximate the "normal" profit level, oligopoly outputs will approximate competitive outputs—they will behave in a manner which, in an otherwise competitive world, would lead to an optimal allocation of resources! However, this suggestion should not be taken very seriously.

[3]We must be careful, however, and heed Professor McKenzie's warning that *proportionality* of prices and marginal costs will not ordinarily produce an optimal resource allocation. This accounts, in part, for the vague terms in which my present discussion is couched. See L. McKenzie, "Ideal Output and the Interdependence of Firms," *Economic Journal*, Vol. LXI, December 1951.

So much for the judgment of oligopoly in a static context. When we include in our evaluation the contribution of oligopoly to economic growth (which will be discussed in Part II of this book) it will be even clearer that the sales maximization hypothesis sheds a favorable light on the effects of oligopolistic organizations on the social welfare. Lest this be taken as apologetics, pure and simple, let me add that the discussion provides no grounds for us to dispense with the services of a vigorous authority charged with enforcement of the antitrust laws in order to prevent the corruption and abuse which can be, and often have been, the fruits of great concentration of economic power.

4. Lump sum taxes

The sales maximization hypothesis has another, rather disturbing, implication for welfare theory. It means that prefixed lump sum ("poll") taxes must lose their convenience for discussions of income redistribution. Even these taxes, like other overheads, can and will be shifted, and their imposition will affect incentives and the allocation of resources.[4] They will be shifted because, when they are levied on him, the oligopolist will raise his prices and reduce his selling costs to a point where his profit constraint is once again satisfied. The explanation of the shiftability of this apparently unshiftable tax is simple—the profit nonmaximizer has a reserve of unclaimed profits to fall back on when he is driven to do so by what he considers to be an unsupportable increase in his costs, though he can do so only at the sacrifice of sales that mean so much to him. Because no one seems to deny that businessmen do, in fact, often raise prices when their overheads increase, this point must be accepted even by someone who questions the sales maximization hypothesis.

5. Implications for monetary and fiscal policy

We have not yet exhausted the diverse areas of economic analysis to which the sales maximization hypothesis can be applied. I shall now indicate its relevance for economic stabilization.

In an important recent contribution,[5] Professor Galbraith has argued that oligopolistic firms are particularly effective conductors of inflationary pressure and are relatively immune to the counterinflationary

---

[4]Note that the hypothesis also requires revision of the usual computation of the shifting and incidence of other taxes on the firm.

[5]J. K. Galbraith, "Market Structure and Stabilization Policy," *Review of Economics and Statistics*, May 1957, especially pp. 127–32.

influences of monetary and fiscal policy. From these results of his analysis he concludes that the efficacy of monetary and fiscal policies depend largely upon their impact on the competitive sectors of the economy that must bear the brunt of the burden of readjustment, and he points out that this raises serious questions about the effectiveness, equity, and wisdom of such policies. In particular, this view suggests that much more extreme monetary and fiscal measures may be required to achieve a given disinflationary effect than we would otherwise have thought to be necessary.

I must differ with Professor Galbraith on a number of these points. I think it can be shown that the difference in role of the competitive and the oligopolistic firm in the inflationary process is not nearly as great as he would have us believe.

To Professor Galbraith, as to many investigators, a prime character-istic of the oligopolistic firm is that it does not normally set a price which maximizes profits. So far I am in agreement. But in his analysis there seems to be no alternative explanation of the price setting process. Somehow, perhaps by historical accident, the price of each item seems to have been set up, and then, for fear of setting off a price war through retaliatory efforts of competitors, the oligopolist apparently never changes such a price unless universal cost changes permit him to do so without being misunderstood by business rivals.

It would be a very odd coincidence indeed if those prices were to happen to lie at their precise profit maximizing levels. In fact, we are told that they will generally lie *below* those that will maximize profits, apparently because inflation calls for rapid upward price shifts as demand increases in monetary terms—price rises greater than those the oligopolist is willing to permit. Furthermore, according to Professor Galbraith, "A commonplace feature of a firm under inflationary demand is a backlog."[6] This backlog, of course, can be eliminated by a price sufficiently high to cut the quantity demanded down to the quantity supplied, but such a price rise the oligopolist presumably refuses to permit.

As a result of all of this, he argues, monetary and fiscal measures may be rendered largely ineffective in the oligopolistic sector. Any rise in costs incurred as a result of interest rate increases need not reduce the oligopolist's profits. Because he is not maximizing his profits to begin with, he can raise his price and increase his profits sufficiently to make up for the higher interest cost. Any reduction in demand pro-duced by such policies may serve only to reduce the backlog of demand and may actually result in no decrease in sales.

[6]*Ibid.*, p. 128.

The oligopolist then, according to Galbraith, will be able to go on as before, with no loss in profits and perhaps no loss in sales. He will have no reason to cut down his investment expenditure. His contribution to inflationary pressure, therefore, will not be diminished unless monetary or fiscal actions are particularly severe.

Such will not be the fate of the competitive small businessman whose prices are fixed on the market and whom rises in costs and cuts in demand really hurt, and hurt at once. Thus, according to Galbraith, besides being less effective than might have been expected, counter-inflationary monetary and fiscal policies can serve to increase industrial concentration and help to contribute to the danger of the decline of the small businessman.

Let us now reexamine these problems with the aid of the sales maximization hypothesis. It follows from this hypothesis that Professor Galbraith is indeed right in asserting that the oligopolist's profits will not normally be maximized. But the reason is not that he is dominated by fear of making price adjustments, although such fears may also play their role. He will fail to maximize profits also because he has another partially overriding purpose to which he is willing to sacrifice some profits.

If this is correct, we must expect only under extraordinary circumstances to encounter the backlog of orders Galbraith considers to be a normal feature of oligopolistic operation during an inflationary period. A firm that tries to maximize dollar sales will not hold back on production that can be sold without price reductions unless either the expansion of its capacity has been unable to keep up with demand or management is so fearful of the future that it hesitates to undertake the required investment commitments.

Consider now the effects on such a firm of a rise in costs that might occur, for example, as the result of an increase in wages or in interest rates. As in Professor Galbraith's analysis, we have seen that this may lead to an increase in the company's selling prices sufficient to prevent any reduction in profits. Otherwise, the rise in costs can reduce the oligopolist's profits below the level he considers to be the minimum under which he can operate. But several other consequences follow from this step.

In the probably more usual case where there is no backlog of orders this price rise must mean some cut in the number of items sold or at least unit sales will not increase as quickly as they otherwise would have. Moreover, if the initial price had been chosen to maximize sales revenues, it is clear that the rise in price must result in a reduction in (or a reduction in the rate of increase of) dollar sales. It follows that:

1. An interest rate or wage increase will also hit the oligopolist where it hurts him—not in his profits but in his sales volume.

2. An interest rate rise need produce no increase in industrial concentration—the oligopolist's sales will decline right along with those of the competitive firm.

3. By reducing the demands for his products or increasing his costs, monetary or fiscal policy can effectively reduce the oligopolist's contribution to inflationary pressure. If his sales fall it will pay him to reduce his demand for factors of production either for immediate use in his manufacturing process or for investment purposes. But this is precisely what a disinflationary monetary and fiscal policy seeks to get him to do.[7]

Thus, in each of these respects I am forced to disagree with Professor Galbraith's policy conclusions. Standard fiscal and monetary measures need not discriminate against competitive firms; they need not promote monopolization, nor are they to be expected to be ineffective in the oligopolistic sectors of the economy.

Even in the case I have not yet discussed, where oligopoly firms have a large backlog of unfilled orders, the Galbraith conclusions can be disputed. If the backlog occurs by design because the oligopolist is afraid of the future and wishes to retain a cushion of demand against contingencies, the rise in price, or the reduction in demand that results from anti-inflation policy will cut down on that cushion. The oligopolist may then be expected to hold back even more in his investment plans, thereby contributing once again to a reduction in inflationary pressure. Similarly, if his backlog of demand piled up because, so to speak, he has been unable to get sufficiently quick delivery on expanded plant and equipment, a reduction in the backlog can mean partial cancellation of investment orders.

Yet there is an important observation I think lies behind Professor Galbraith's discussion. In times of inflation it is true that the firm can frequently raise prices in response to cost changes and get away with little or no observable ill effect. What occurs here is that the cost rise, because it is universal, provides the purchasing power that permits consumers to buy as much as they did before the price rise. This is the mechanism of the familiar wage-price spiral.

[7]Incidentally, I must take exception to Galbraith's assertion that "firms in the oligopolistic sector have the opportunity of offsetting any credit restrictions to which they are subject by increasing their prices and their earned resources and devoting them to investment," p. 131. It can take several years of increased accumulation out of profits to offset a large reduction in credit. Hence, this means may well be insufficient to prevent forced *postponement* of oligopolistic investment, which is all the deflationary effect that is usually sought.

But here the competitive firm is in no worse a strategic position than is the oligopolist. The demand for the small businessman's products will be raised by increases in wages, whether his own or the oligopolist's. Thus, the competitive firm is able to participate wholeheartedly in the inflationary process just as is the oligopolist. Indeed, it may almost be suspected that the small firm will in this respect occupy the slightly better position. For in competitive markets the translation of increased costs into higher prices is rapid, impersonal, and automatic. To the extent that the large firm hesitates to change prices even in the upward direction, it may therefore be placed at a relative disadvantage.

Of course, rises in interest rates differ from wage rises in that they do not all go into increases in money income in the hands of the public. A large proportion of higher interest payments may represent a transfer to banks and insurance companies where they will not immediately be used to swell the monetary demand for commodities. That is essentially why interest rate increases can act as an offset to inflationary pressures, while wage rises do not ordinarily do so. But if interest rate rises do prevent increases in demand, they will do so equally for the oligopolist and for the small firm.

I am not to be interpreted to hold the position that different monetary and fiscal policies all, and always, fall with exactly equal weight on the competitive and oligopolistic sectors of the economy. Clearly this need not be so. It depends on costs structures, the relative elasticities of demands for the products of the two sectors, and many other considerations. My position is just that the relative effects can only be determined after far more careful and detailed investigation of their product lines and related matters and that I will be very surprised should such an investigation show that all the tools of monetary and fiscal policy consistently favor either group against the other.

PART II

ON THE THEORY OF
ECONOMIC GROWTH

CHAPTER 9

Introduction to part II

In a recent work,[1] Professor Haavelmo calls attention to the relative lack of theoretical literature dealing with "phenomena like that of neighboring countries whose standards of living have remained at strikingly different levels for centuries . . . countries where income per head has doubled or tripled during the last hundred years while in others there has been only slight progress, or stagnation."[2] This part of my book is an attempt at a direct answer to Haavelmo's appeal. Of necessity, the model developed will only produce the conclusions that have been built into it. Yet, I hope that the very simplicity of the construction that is finally employed will help persuade the reader of its relevance to the problems of economic development.

1. The goals of development

By and large, specification of the goals to be pursued by a development program are best left to be formulated case by case. Nevertheless, it is useful, at least for expository purposes, to specify a broad objective.

Largely as a matter of convenience, I shall consider real per capita national income the item to be maximized and say that the lower that figure, the more underdeveloped the region. This choice is somewhat

[1]T. Haavelmo, *A Study in the Theory of Economic Evolution*, Amsterdam, North-Holland Publishing, 1954.

[2]*Ibid.*, p. 4. Haavelmo contrasts the lack of writing in this area with the abundance of "books analysing short-run equilibria, or the 'catastrophies' of ten per cent dents in the national income of the more advanced, industrialized countries." Perhaps as bait to potential writers on economic development he adds, "I would venture the guess that there is really a much better chance of significant econometric results if we turn to theories that have as their objects of explanation the really big dissimilarities in economic life. Thus, if we have, side-by-side, two large economic regions of which one has a per capita national product several times as big as the other, there must be a tremendous—and therefore presumably detectable—difference in the 'causal factors' at work in the two cases," p. 5.

arbitrary.[3] It may not represent the goals of the politician in the under-developed area for whom industrialization for its own sake or (because of its military significance) *total* national income or a variety of other desiderata may be more important. Moreover, inhabitants of the area in question may not consider development in this, or any other sense, to be particularly desirable.[4] Certainly I do not believe that there exists any set of overriding ethical principles that calls categorically for development programs.

2. Outline of Part II

The next chapter returns to our model of the oligopolistic firm in an attempt to extend the Schumpeterian analysis of the growth mechanism in modern capitalist economies. By examining the process whereby others have succeeded in growing rapidly, it may be possible for the development planner to learn how much of the mechanism can be adapted for use by those economies whose expansion has been modest.

I shall argue that there exist in our economy powerful institutional forces making for economic growth that appear to be absent in under-developed regions. This suggests that it is not enough to set up programs designed to increase productive *capacity* in underdeveloped areas—programs involving the import of capital and improved education, nutrition, and medical care to increase the quality of the labor force. Without at the same time introducing strong driving forces analogous with those that direct our own economic capacities toward the promotion of growth, rather than to some other purposes, the underdeveloped areas may fall further behind rather than narrowing the gap between themselves and the Western capitalist world.

In examining the forces that make for growth in our economy, I maintain that at least some of them lie deep in our institutional structure—the nature of business goals and of the competitive process and the characteristics of corporate enterprise. At best, such institutions, by their very nature, can be introduced and developed only very slowly in the underdeveloped areas. Indeed, we cannot be confident that they bear transplanting at all. We simply do not know enough about the working of men's minds and the mores rooted in them to be sure how to go about creating the appropriate psychological climate.

[3]But *cf.* Jacob Viner, *International Trade and Economic Development*, Glencoe, The Free Press, 1952, pp. 94–101.

[4]There are even cases where primitive populations are apparently not convinced of the desirability of increased output. But I suspect that, by and large, the view that many primitive peoples are uninterested in their material rewards is an exaggeration. See Ch. 13 in this book.

This conclusion, by itself, is not very encouraging to development planners, but hope can be drawn from another quarter. The phenomenal growth of the Soviet economy indicates that it is possible to find effective substitutes for the slow transmutation of men's attitudes and social institutions. Unfortunately, of course, the totalitarian techniques employed are as distasteful to most of us as is the prospect of continued poverty in so many regions.

This book ends, therefore, with a policy proposal which seeks to extract the best of both the Soviet and the Western examples, the first of which involved the rapid introduction of a powerful motor mechanism capable of producing a tremendous acceleration in the level of national output, and the second of which has been characterized by the employment of no more coercion than is part and parcel of the normal operation of democratic government. As far as I know the proposal is novel and, for that reason alone, its practicality is suspect—no one may have bothered to formulate such a scheme before because no one has thought it worth the trouble. Whether this is so the reader will have to judge for himself. In any event, the suggestion is not put forth as a cure-all. It will leave unsolved many crucial problems, such as rapid population growth, inadequacy of natural resources, nutrition, and medicine, and others, all of whose importance for development should not be underestimated. But I think the proposal does promise to provide a strong mechanism without which substantial increases in growth are likely to be impossible and which can render more tractable the other problems of economic development.

CHAPTER 10

Growth in the activity of the firm*

From our static model of decision-making by the economy's larger firms we turn now to the structure of the company's growth decision process. We will consider on what basis management determines how rapidly to expand its outputs and its activities generally. In the course of the discussion we shall see how a conventional profit maximization approach can serve as the basis for a growth equilibrium decision model and how one can extend the static model of the firm to deal with problems of considerable importance to management. We will also examine what differences may be produced by management's choice of objectives. The discussion undertakes to shed some light on the origin and determination of the profit constraint that plays so important a role in the sales maximization model of Chapter 7. But, above all, the chapter is designed to argue that the extraordinary long-term growth record of the Western capitalist economies can to a considerable extent be ascribed to the motivation for growth in the business firm. It will be shown that any of a variety of plausible company objectives can call for a considerable rate of business expansion, either as an end in itself or as an essential instrument for the achievement of the goals of the firm. This is the primary purpose of the growth-equilibrium model to which we now turn.

1. A profit-maximizing–growth-equilibrium model

In the ordinary static model of the firm, once the optimal or profit maximizing output level has been determined, the firm will be motivated to continue to produce this quantity in perpetuity. The level of output

*I must express my thanks for permission to reproduce in this chapter portions of two articles: to the editors of the *American Economic Review* for passages from my "The Theory of Expansion of the Firm," which appeared in Vol. LII, December 1962, pp. 1078–87; and to Richard D. Irwin, Inc., for a passage from my chapter entitled "Company Goals, Growth, and the Multiproduct Firm," in Reavis Cox, Wroe Alderson, and Stanley J. Shapiro, eds., *Theory in Marketing*, Second Series, Homewood, Ill., Richard D. Irwin, Inc., for the American Marketing Association, 1964.

will not change until some fortuitous circumstance causes a shift in consumer attitudes or in technology that modifies the cost or demand structure and makes some alternative production level more profitable. Thus, once the equilibrium level of output is found, the operation of the firm can be considered a routine exercise. There is no really essential decision-making role to be performed by management so long as market conditions and technology remain the same.

However, economists who have spent time observing the operations of business enterprises come away impressed with the extent of management's preoccupation with growth. Expansion is a theme that (with some variations) is dinned into the ears of stockholders and is constantly reported in the financial pages and the journals devoted to business affairs. Indeed, in talking to business executives one may easily come to believe that the growth of the firm is the main preoccupation of top management. A stationary optimum would doubtless be abhorrent to the captains of industry, whose main concern is surely not at what size their enterprises should finally settle down (except where sheer size endangers their standing with the administrators of the antitrust laws) but rather how rapidly to grow.

Although the static theory of the firm is a helpful snapshot description of a system in motion,[1] it is useful also to have an alternative construction of the kind described in this chapter—another equilibrium analysis in which the *rate of growth* of output, rather than its *level*, is the variable whose value is determined by optimality considerations.

For simplicity, our first growth model is confined to a case in which input and output prices are fixed (pure competition) and where the production function is linear and homogeneous. With constant returns to scale and constant prices there would seem to be no economic bounds to the firm's output. If production level Q is profitable, output kQ must be k times as profitable because costs and revenues each must have risen exactly k times. This would seem to force us to the ludicrous conclusion that management should in these circumstances expand its output without limit and that it should presumably do so immediately.[2]

---

[1]Thus, I am emphatically *not* proposing that the conventional theory of the firm be relegated to the garbage heap or the museum of curious antiquities. Static analysis of a nonstationary phenomenon can be immensely illuminating, and the received theory of the firm contains many very helpful results, both from the point of view of the understanding of the workings of the economy and the applied work of the operations researcher. It would be folly to deny ourselves the use of this body of analysis just because its domain of applicability is somewhat limited.

[2]This is closely related to a well-known argument of Kaldor's. See N. Kaldor, "The Equilibrium of the Firm," *Economic Journal*, Vol. XLIV, March 1934, reprinted in N. Kaldor, *Essays in Value and Distribution*, Glencoe, The Free Press, 1961.

There are several fairly obvious reasons why things do not work out this way in practice.

First, sheer construction costs involved in providing physical facilities increase disproportionately as expansion is accelerated. If it normally takes two years to complete the erection of a certain type of factory, a crash program to get it finished in one year is likely to be far more expensive, and any attempt to build many factories of the same sort at once is very likely to strain the capacity of those who construct them and so may add substantially to costs.

A second reason for increasing costs of expansion is financial. The capital market that faces any one company is usually far from perfect. As the company's demand for funds increases, it is likely to find that the cost it must pay for them goes up. The amount of expansion that can be financed out of retained earnings is limited. Too large an issue of new stocks or bonds will drive down the price significantly, and financial institutions may place absolute limits on the amounts they are willing to lend or will increase their lending only if they are offered extremely attractive terms.

Third, there is an internal limitation to expansion: the fact that administrative and organizational costs are almost certain to rise disproportionately with the rate of expansion of the firm. As the growth of the company increases, managerial capacity must also expand. Members must be added to the executive group, and there must be time for their training and opportunities for them to acquire experience. [3]

Fourth, investment in expansion is an inherently risky proposition— a venture into markets whose potential is never fully known. The cost of this risk will tend to rise with the proportion of the company's funds committed to growth. All of this means that costs are virtually certain to be a function, and a sharply rising function, of the firm's rate of growth. This is illustrated in Figure 10.1, where the total cost curve

---

Here the author reminded us that equilibrium of the competitive firm requires some sort of increasing costs to make it unprofitable for the company to expand indefinitely. But under pure competition there seems to be no obvious source of diminishing returns and, hence, little reason for *any* scale of operations of the competitive firm to constitute a long-run stationary equilibrium situation.

[3] "In numerous companies ... the volume of new profitable investment opportunities being turned up is substantially larger than can be handled with the company's management organization and staff. Too rapid growth has proved embarrassing in the past, as a result of excessive strain on other parts of the organization, or because of loss of customer good will or other unhappy developments attributable to undigestable rates of expansion." Lintner, "Effect of Corporate Taxation . . . ," *op. cit.* p. 528. *Cf.* also S. Melman, "The Rise of Administrative Overhead in the Manufacturing Industries of the United States 1899–1947," *Oxford Economic Papers*, Vol. III, February 1951, and E. Penrose, "Limits to the Growth and Size of Firms," *American Economic Review*, Vol. XLV, May 1955.

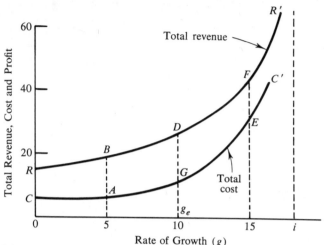

FIG. 10.1

rises more rapidly as we move from left to right. That is, as the firm considers a rate of growth of 5 or 10 or 15 percent, management is confronted with the fact that its total costs at a 15 percent rate of growth will be far higher than those that would apply if a 10 percent rate of growth were decided upon.

Total revenue, which may be defined as the discounted present value of the future stream of returns, is also a rising function of rate of growth. That is, a company that selects a more rapid rate of growth over its lifetime may expect higher receipts than one which chooses to expand more slowly.

Now it will be observed in Figure 10.1 that total profits first increase and then decrease as we move toward the right. That is, GD is larger than AB but EF is smaller than GD. This means that there will be an optimal (profit-maximizing) rate of growth for the firm described in this diagram. But it is the *rate of expansion* of the firm's output rather than the *level* of its production that is to be determined by this equilibrium analysis. Each company will find it unprofitable to expand either too slowly or too quickly, and there will be a rate of expansion (in the case of the diagram, 10 percent) that makes a maximal contribution to the company's long-run profits.

Thus, in the model described in Figure 10.1, firms grow not *despite* the effect of expansion on profits but *because* such growth makes the firm more profitable. Growth occurs and continues out of the very logic of the analysis and not as a result of some appendages subsequently imposed upon the model.

2. Formalization of the growth-equilibrium model

This model employs several specific assumptions: first, that management considers only a very simple growth pattern—a fixed percentage rate of growth, to be continued into the indefinite future. This heroic assumption is adopted to permit a simple characterization of the optimal growth path by means of a single variable, the permanent percentage rate of growth, g.[4] Second, it is also assumed, at least for the moment, that the company's objective (which determines the optimal rate of growth of its output) is conventional profit maximization. Finally, it is posited that costs can be divided into two categories: ordinary production and operating costs and costs that arise only as a result of the expansion process. Any costs that would be associated with a given level of output if the output rate were not changing may be classed under output costs; any additional outlays above and beyond the output costs are called expansion costs. Output costs will only be taken into account implicitly, in the net revenue figures. That is, in discussing revenues, net revenue figures from which output costs have already been deducted will be employed.

Let R represent the initial net revenue of our firm, g be the rate of growth (which is to be determined), and i be the rate of interest relevant in discounting future revenues. Thus, i is the company's "cost of capital"—which is likely to be considerably higher than any more or less pure interest rate such as the rate on any class of government bonds. Then, because of the constancy of the prices of all of the firm's inputs and outputs and the linear homogeneity of the production function, net revenues will grow precisely in the same proportion as inputs. In t periods, the firm's net revenue will be $R(1 + g)^t$, and the discounted present value of that net revenue will be $R[(1 + g)/(1 + i)]^t$. The present value of the expected stream of revenues therefore will be:

$$P = \sum_{t=0}^{\infty} R \left(\frac{1 + g}{1 + i} \right)^t$$

$$(10.1) \qquad = R \frac{1}{1 - [(1 + g)/(1 + i)]} = R \frac{1 + i}{i - g}$$

provided only[5] that $g < i$, so that $(1 + g)/(1 + i) < 1$, as is required for convergence of the geometric series (10.1).

---

[4]If this premise is not employed and the optimal rate of growth at every future moment of time is left to be determined, we are forced into the morass of the theory of functionals, and we cannot escape without at least some recourse to the calculus of variations.

[5]The problems caused for such a model if the rate of growth exceeds the rate of interest are well known. Specifically, the geometric series (10.1) will then not converge

It is perfectly obvious in this situation that we have

(10.2) $\quad \dfrac{\partial P}{\partial g} > 0,$

that is, the present value of the net revenue stream will grow indefinitely with the rate of expansion g. In fact, P will grow at an increasing rate with g, and its value will exceed any preassigned number as g approaches i, as is shown in the net revenue curve, RR', in Figure 10.1. There is nothing here, then, to place a limit on the rate of expansion of the firm.

As we have just seen, the firm will be constrained from accelerating its activities without limit by its expansion costs, the present value of which we designate $C(g)$. It may be expected that after some point the resulting increases in costs will catch up with the marginal revenues derived from more rapid expansion.[6] That is, it may be assumed that the slope of the cost curve CC', which is the graph of the function $C(g)$, will normally be less than that of RR' near the horizontal axis, but that eventually the slope of the former will catch up with and finally exceed that of the latter. (It may be, however, that in some cases the slope of the cost curve will exceed that of the revenue curve throughout the

---

and the present value of the firm's profit stream will no longer be finite. See, e.g., D. Durand, "Growth Stocks and the Petersburgh Paradox," *Journal of Finance*, Vol. XII, September 1957. However, as Miller and Modigliani have shown, the case $g > i$ is not a serious possibility. They write: "Although the case of (perpetual) growth rates greater than the discount factor is the much-discussed 'growth stock paradox' . . . it has no real economic significance . . . . This will be apparent when one recalls that the discount rate . . . though treated as a constant in partial equilibrium (relative price) analysis of the kind presented here, is actually a variable from the standpoint of the system as a whole. That is, if the assumption of finite value for all shares did not hold, because for some shares g was (perpetually) greater than i, then i would necessarily rise until an over-all equilibrium in the capital markets had been restored." M. H. Miller and F. Modigliani, "Dividend Policy, Growth and the Valuation of Shares," *Journal of Business*, Vol. XXXIV, October 1961, fn. 14. (The notation has been changed from the original to that employed here.)

An alternative way of avoiding this problem is to drop the (unrealistic) premise that the horizon is infinite. However, a finite horizon (say, one involving five periods) will yield an expression for total revenue that is somewhat more messy than (10.1). Though it will be a fifth-degree polynomial, it will have only positive coefficients, and so any equilibrium still will be unique. Indeed, the results of the infinite horizon model all seem to continue to hold in the finite horizon case.

[6]This view of the shape of the cost function can also be defended with the aid of the usual (somewhat shaky) appeal to the second-order maximum conditions, for given the shape of our revenue function, the cost curve must behave in the manner shown in Fig. 10.1 or there would be no profit-maximizing growth rate.

Note also that C is likely to be a function of other variables in addition to g, i.e., it is apt to depend on the initial absolute level of output. A small firm will perhaps find it less costly to expand at a rate of 10 percent than will a large company.

positive quadrant so that the optimal growth rate will be zero or negative.)

Specifically, we obtain the growth-profit function:

$$(10.3) \quad \Pi = P - C(g) = R\frac{1+i}{i-g} - C(g).$$

The profit-maximizing conditions are then (using the notation Π_g for $\partial\Pi/\partial g$, etc.)

$$(10.4) \quad \Pi_g = P_g - C'(g) = R\frac{1+i}{(i-g)^2} - C'(g) = 0,$$

(the first-order marginal revenue equals marginal cost condition) and

$$(10.5) \quad \Pi_{gg} \doteq 2R\frac{1+i}{(i-g)^3} - C''(g) < 0$$

(the second-order condition).

Graphically, the equilibrium rate of growth is given by Og_e in Figure 10.1, the value at which the slope of the expansion cost curve CC' and that of RR' are equal.[7]

3. Digression: comparative statics in the analysis of the model[8]

This simple growth model can easily be made to yield some results in terms of comparative statics. While some of these results are not particularly surprising, they may offer some reassurance that the model does not possess particularly perverse properties and that it can serve as an instrument of analysis much like the standard stationary equilibrium model.

First, a rise in the interest rate will reduce the present value of the stream of expected revenues, for we have[9] by (10.1)

$$(10.6) \quad P_i = R\frac{(i-g)-(1+i)}{(i-g)^2} = -R\frac{1+g}{(i-g)^2} < 0.$$

---

[7]We might even envision a long-run zero-profit competitive growth equilibrium in which entry has caused shifting of the RR' and CC' curves and produced a zero-profit tangency position at which growth rate has settled. There is some question in my mind whether, in a growth model such as this, much relevance can be ascribed to that type of long-run adjustment.

[8]Because the mathematics employed in this section are a bit more demanding than those used in the remainder of the book and, because in any event the content of the section is not directly relevant to the main theme of the volume, some readers may prefer to omit it.

[9]A complication is introduced by the fact that interest payments are among the output costs which have been subtracted from our net revenue figure R, so that R should no longer be treated as a constant when differentiating with respect to i. This

Moreover, a rise in the interest rate will reduce the *marginal* revenue yield of increased economic growth, P_g, for we have, differentiating (10.6) partially with respect to g,

$$(10.7) \quad P_{ig} = P_{gi} = -R\frac{(i - g)^2 + 2(i - g)(1 + g)}{(i - g)^4} < 0$$

by our basic assumption $g < i$.

It is now rather simple to prove that (at least in a perfect capital market where some market rate of interest determines the relevant discount factor) a rise in the interest rate will reduce the equilibrium rate of growth of the firm. Differentiating the first-order maximum condition (10.4) totally and setting $d\Pi_g = 0$ (so that the equilibrium condition continues to hold) we obtain:

$$d\Pi_g = P_{gi}di + \Pi_{gg}\, dg = 0$$

or

$$(10.8) \quad \frac{dg}{di} = -\frac{P_{gi}}{\Pi_{gg}} < 0$$

by (10.5) and (10.7).

Geometrically, this obvious result is a consequence of the fact that a rise in i reduces the slope of the RR' curve in Figure 10.1 throughout its length, as indicated by (10.7), so that the equilibrium growth level, Og_e, must move to the left.

A somewhat more interesting application arises out of some recent proposals to stimulate business growth by means of appropriate government subsidies.[10] Suppose one is considering two alternative subsidy plans for this purpose. The first plan involves payments (S_{1t}) proportionate with the percentage rate of the increase of the firm's output:

$$S_{1t} = s_1 g_t = s_1 g.$$

The present value of all such expected future subsidy payments is

$$(10.9) \quad S_1 = s_1 g \sum_{t=0}^{\infty}\left(\frac{1}{1 + i}\right)^t = s_1 g\left(1 + \frac{1}{i}\right).$$

---

can be taken care of by noting that our assumptions of linear homogeneity and constant price imply that the quantity of money capital employed by the firm should be strictly proportionate with $R(1 + g)^t$. Say it will equal $kR(1 + g)^t$ and therefore incur an annual interest payment $ikR(1 + g)^t$. In that case we need merely write $R = R^*(1 - ik)$ and make this substitution in our revenue function (10.1). It may then easily be verified by direct differentiation that the resulting expression for P_i will be slightly more complicated than (10.6) but that it will still be negative. A similar remark holds for (10.7) and (10.8).

[10]For example, in the Kennedy Administration 1961 investment credit proposals. See also Canadian House of Commons, *Proceedings*, April 10, 1962, and Ch. 15 in this book.

The alternative plan proposes to offer a stream of subsidies (S_{2t}) proportional to the absolute rate of increase of output:

$$S_{2t} = s_2[R(1 + g)^t - R(1 + g)^{t-1}] = s_2gR(1 + g)^{t-1}$$

whose capitalized present value is:

$$S_2 = \frac{s_2gR}{1 + g} \sum_{t=1}^{\infty} \left(\frac{1 + g}{1 + i}\right)^t = \frac{s_2gR}{1 + g} \left\{\left[\sum_{t=0}^{\infty} \left(\frac{1 + g}{1 + i}\right)^t\right] - 1\right\}$$

$$= \frac{s_2gR}{1 + g} \left(\frac{1 + i}{i - g} - 1\right) = \frac{s_2gR}{1 + g} \cdot \frac{1 + g}{i - g}$$

or

$$(10.10) \quad S_2 = \frac{s_2gR}{i - g}.$$

Adding, in turn, the subsidy expressions (10.9) and (10.10) to our basic profit function (10.3) we obtain the two new profit expressions:

$$(10.11) \quad \Pi^* = R\frac{1 + i}{i - g} - C(g) + s_1g\left(1 + \frac{1}{i}\right)$$

and

$$(10.12) \quad \Pi^{**} = R\frac{1 + i}{i - g} - C(g) + \frac{s_2gR}{i - g}.$$

By the same procedure as was employed when the effect of an interest rate change was examined, we arrive at the respective comparative statics results:

$$(10.13) \quad \frac{dg}{ds_1} = -\frac{1 + 1/i}{\Pi^*_{gg}} > 0$$

and

$$(10.14) \quad \frac{dg}{ds_2} = -\frac{iR}{\Pi^{**}_{gg}(i - g)^2} > 0$$

if the second-order conditions $\Pi^*_{gg} < 0$ and $\Pi^{**}_{gg} < 0$ both hold. Thus, both types of subsidy indeed would stimulate the growth of the profit-maximizing firm.

We can go beyond this somewhat uninteresting conclusion by asking which of these two types of subsidy will yield more growth per dollar of government outlay. For this purpose we must deal not with s_1 and s_2, the subsidy rates, but with the total subsidy outlays, S_1 and S_2, as given by (10.9) and (10.10). From these we obtain:

(10.15) $\dfrac{ds_1}{dS_1} = \dfrac{1}{g(1 + 1/i)}$

and

(10.16) $\dfrac{ds_2}{dS_2} = \dfrac{i - g}{Rg}$.

Multiplying (10.13) by (10.15) and (10.14) by (10.16) and writing out the expressions for Π_{gg}^* and Π_{gg}^{**} we obtain:

(10.17) $\dfrac{dg}{dS_1} = - \dfrac{1}{g\Pi_{gg}^*} = - \dfrac{1}{g\{2R[(1 + i)/(i - g)^3] - C''(g)\}}$

and

(10.18)

$$\dfrac{dg}{dS_2} = - \dfrac{i}{g(i - g)\Pi_{gg}^{**}}$$

$$= - \dfrac{i}{g\{2R(1 + i)/(i - g)^3 - C''(g) + [2is_2R/(i - g)^3]\}(i - g)}.$$

Hence, subsidy S_2 will yield higher marginal returns than subsidy S_1 if and only if expression (10.18) exceeds expression (10.17), that is, if and only if

$$- \dfrac{1}{g\Pi_{gg}^*} < - \dfrac{i}{g(i - g)\{\Pi_{gg}^* + [2is_2R/(i - g)^3]\}}.$$

This requires

$$(i - g)\left[\Pi_{gg}^* + \dfrac{2is_2R}{(i - g)^3}\right] > i\Pi_{gg}^*$$

or

$$- g\Pi_{gg}^* + (i - g)\dfrac{2is_2R}{(i - g)^3} > 0$$

and (because $\Pi_{gg}^* < 0$ by the second-order condition) since both terms in this last expression are positive, this requirement will always be satisfied. We conclude, then, that in our model a subsidy of the second type will always yield higher marginal growth returns than a subsidy of the first type.

It is also noteworthy that a net investment tax credit of the sort originally proposed is essentially equivalent in our model to a growth subsidy proposal of type two, for the investment credit is a subsidy proportionate to the level of net investment. With our linear homogeneous production function, and with constant input prices, the capital-output ratio will be constant, so that a subsidy proportionate to investment automatically will be proportional to the absolute rate of increase in output.

Because so many other considerations must enter any decision among alternative growth stimulation methods, there is no point in laboring this discussion further. The case serves, however, to illustrate how meaningful theorems can be derived from the growth-equilibrium model of the firm.

4. Alternative company objectives[11]

The discussion so far has been confined to the case of pure competition and has assumed that the firm's objective is to maximize profit. But larger *oligopolistic* firms may well have a different set of objectives. Specifically, I have suggested earlier in this book that management's goal may well be to maximize sales (total revenue) subject to a profit constraint. Though I remain firmly convinced of the merit of the hypothesis as a static characterization of the current facts of oligopolistic business operation, in the present context—a growth equilibrium analysis—it is desirable to modify the hypothesis in two respects.

First, maximization of *rate of growth* of sales revenue seems a somewhat better approximation to the goals of many management groups in large firms than is maximization of the current *level* of sales. For example, most company publicity materials seem to emphasize the extent to which the firm has "progressed" rather than the sheer magnitude of its current operations. In my earlier static model I was forced to employ a sales-level objective as an approximation to a measure of the rate of growth of the firm's scale of operations. A growth-equilibrium model now frees me from this necessity.

The second modification deals with the nature of the profit constraint, which in a static model may have seemed to be arbitrarily imposed from the outside—perhaps even a device to avoid explaining what had to be explained, very much like the fixed mark-up of doubtful origin which lies at the heart of the full-cost pricing discussions. A multiperiod analysis in which growth is taken into account enables me to give an explanation of the profit constraint which, I hope, is somewhat less superficial and rather more convincing.

From a long-run point of view, profit no longer acts as a constraint in the calculations of the sales maximizer or the growth maximizer. Rather, it is an instrumental variable—a means whereby management

[11]For a different view on some of the discussion that follows see J. Williamson, "Profit, Growth, and Sales Maximization," *Economica*, Vol. XXXIII, New Series, February 1966.

works toward its goals. Specifically, profits are a means for obtaining capital needed to finance expansion plans. Capital is raised both by direct retention of profits and by the payment of dividends to induce outside investors to provide funds to the company. But, beyond some point, profits compete with sales. The lower prices and higher marketing outlays necessary to promote sales also cut into net earnings. Hence, too high a level of profits will reduce the magnitude of the firm's current operations, while too low a profit level will prevent future growth. The optimal profit stream will be that intermediate stream consistent with the largest flow of output (or rate of growth of output) over the firm's lifetime.

Because I have no desire to argue that all firms are united in their choice of objective or to deny that the goals of management are subject to change with the passage of time, it seems desirable to consider a variety of possible company objectives rather than just sales growth maximization. For this purpose one may utilize a set of relationships such as the following:

$$(10.19) \quad \Pi = f(R, g, i)$$

$$(10.20) \quad S = \Sigma_t R \left(\frac{1 + g}{1 + i}\right)^t = R \left(\frac{1 + i}{i - g}\right) \quad \text{[by (10.1)]}$$

$$(10.21) \quad g = G(I, R)$$

$$(10.22) \quad I \leqq F(\Pi)$$

where Π is the present value of the stream of total company profits, S is the present value of the stream of expected sales (here we drop our earlier assumption that these are net of output costs), R is the initial level of sales, i is the company's discount rate, assumed to be a known constant, g is the rate of growth of company output, and I is the present value of investment, that is, the *total* money capital invested by the firm.

Equation (10.19) shows the dependence of profits on the growth rate and the initial sales level. It is the same as Equation (10.3) but utilizes slightly more general notation. Specifically, the function f in (10.19) behaves in the manner illustrated in Figure 10.1, so that at sufficiently large values of g profits may be expected to decline.

Equation (10.20) simply defines S as the discounted present value of long-run sales. Equation (10.21) describes the dependence of growth rate on the firm's level of investment, including research outlays as well as expenditures on capital utilizing current technology. It also takes into account the investment outlay required for current sales, R, thus expressing the competition of R and g for company funds. Finally, inequality (10.22) is a financial constraint indicating that the amount of money available to the firm is dependent on its expected profits.[12]

The firm may now be taken alternatively to maximize Π, g, S, or R or perhaps some combination (say, some sort of weighted average) of their values, with some or all of the other relationships serving as constraints. Profit maximization, for example, would take (10.19) as its objective function with (10.21) and (10.22) serving as constraints, whereas growth maximization would take (10.21) as its maximum with (10.19) and (10.22) as its constraints.

A diagrammatic depiction of this model perhaps can make clearer the nature of the relationships. It can also suggest the qualitative consequences of pursuit of alternative objectives. In particular, it will indicate that the goals are inherently independent—that attainment of any one of the four objectives does not imply that any of the others need simultaneously be achieved.

Figure 10.2 is a three-dimensional diagram representing (10.19), (10.21), and (10.22), with the axes indicating values of g, R, and Π. The domelike shaded figure is the profit function (10.19), whose location and shape will vary with the value of i. We have already seen why after some point Π will begin to decline with further increases in g. Similarly, in accord with the standard assumptions of static theory we would expect that profit would ultimately begin to decline with excessive current sales, that is, with increases in R. Equations (10.21) and (10.22) have been combined to yield a relationship $\Pi \geq \phi(g, R)$ indicating the minimal profit level necessary to provide the finance requisite for any given combination of g and R. For simplicity this finance requirement is represented in the diagram by a plane $I'I''I'''I$ that slopes upward as we move away from the origin, thus implying that more financing is needed to attain larger values of g and R. As drawn, the plane does not go through the origin, indicating that some funds are needed even by a firm that is not expanding. We note that the only feasible g and R combinations are those corresponding to points inside the intersection of this plane with the profit surface, that is, points lying inside the curve labeled "growth possibility boundary." For only at such points are company profits at least as high as the amount needed to finance the g, R combination represented; that is, everywhere else the profit surface lies below the finance requirement locus.

---

[12]The precise form of the relationship does not matter for present purposes, though I take the available I to be an increasing function of Π. This certainly seems to accord with the conclusions of both the theoretical and the descriptive literature of corporation finance.

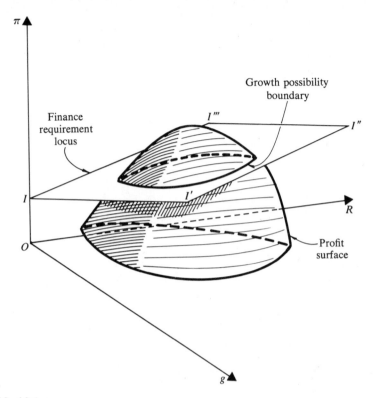

FIG. 10.2

Contour lines are used to collapse Figure 10.2 into a two-dimensional diagram in Figure 10.3. This figure shows the growth possibility boundary crossing the R axis but not the g axis. This means that the firm can survive financially with zero growth but not with zero sales. This latter graph also shows the set of (long-run) iso-sales loci obtained from (10.20) by setting $R(1 + i)/(i - g) = k$ (constant). These are the linear relations $R = -kg/(1 + i) + ki/(1 + i)$ whose slope is clearly negative and all of which have the g intercept $g = i$.

In this diagram only profit maximization occurs in the interior of the feasible region, at the point Π_{max}. Growth maximization occurs at the most rightward point on the growth possibility boundary; the R_{max} point occupies the highest point on the boundary, while S_{max} is given by the point of tangency between the boundary and an iso-sales line. The figure shows at once that S_{max} is not generally consistent with R_{max} or g_{max}, as some of my correspondents have suggested. Indeed, it

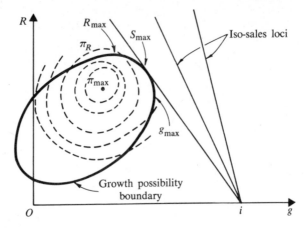

FIG. 10.3

is seen that all the objectives we have considered can be mutually inconsistent.

Figure 10.3 also shows more clearly the nature of the profit constraint and the dependence of the minimal acceptable profit level upon the choice of a long-run company objective. To illustrate the point, if the company desires to achieve maximal R, this yields for the static model a profit constraint of the form $\Pi \geq \Pi_R$ in accord with the iso-profit curve, Π_R passing through point R_{max}. To maximize current R one is forced to choose values of g and hence Π that provide the finance necessary to achieve R_{max}.

Finally, and for our purposes most important, we consider the value of g corresponding to each of our four objectives.[13] In each case we see that a very substantial rate of growth may be required even if growth is not among the company's objectives. Though the company may seek ultimately to maximize sales volume, current or future, or may be

[13]If we write g_{Π}, g_R, g_S, and g_g for the rates of growth corresponding to maximal Π, R, S, and g respectively, it is obvious that g_g must always be greater than or equal to any of the others. We will also have $g_S \geq g_{\Pi}$ because by (10.3) and (10.20) $\Pi = S - C(g) - \phi(S)$, where $\phi(S)$ is the ordinary production cost associated with sales volume S. But S increases with g for any level of i and R, so that we would expect both $\phi(S)$ and $C(g)$, the expansion cost, to increase monotonically with g, and the result follows. Similarly, we must have $g_S \geq g_R$ because by (10.20) for any given R, $\partial S/\partial g > 0$. This can also be seen from Figure 10.3 where R_{max} will always occur at the maximal point where the growth possibility boundary is horizontal, while S_{max} will occur at a point on the northeastern portion of the boundary where its slope is negative (since the iso-sales locus to which it is tangent must be of negative slope). There seems, however, to be no necessary relationship between the magnitudes of g_{Π} and g_R.

interested primarily in profits, a considerable rate of growth may plausibly be expected to serve its interests. Even maximization of R, the *current* value of sales, may require a sizable rate of expansion, for that helps to provide the prospective profits needed to acquire the financing utilized by R_{max}. Thus, in an economy such as ours the business firm is seen to be a source and, it seems plausible, a very important source, of the economy's drive for expansion.

5. Contagion in company expansion

Management usually keeps its eye not only on the absolute magnitude of its operations, but also on their relationship to the levels of achievement of other firms in its group. Market share, for example, seems to be one of the barometers most widely utilized by businessmen. The result is that one firm's growth begets another's.

In fact, management is not ordinarily content to play a passive role in the growth process; that is, it is not prepared to wait for fortuitous events to impose growth upon it. The businessman understands thoroughly the nature of the battle for market share. He realizes that sooner or later someone will grow and he will then be forced to fight to maintain his firm's relative position. How much more satisfactory it is to grow first, especially because it is then possible to choose one's own timing strategy. Rather than waiting passively for someone to make a first move, anticipation leads firms to undertake active programs of expansion, and the desire to maintain market share renders these programs contagious.[14]

6. Motivation for "orderly" growth

Because the typical oligopolistic firm is a conglomeration of heterogeneous enterprises, it can offset their risks against one another on the familiar insurance principle. This means that the oligopolist can better afford to go where the competitor must fear to tread. He is well equipped to undertake the innovation and investment that produce economic growth.

However, there is another side to this picture. With the development of the corporate form of organization the vast body of stockholders

[14]". . . in progressive industries, vigorous competitors will be basing their judgement on what they think (or what they are afraid) other leading firms are (or may be) going to do—not simply on what they have already done except insofar as a vigorous, progressive past is properly extrapolated to the future. One or a few firms 'hell-bent for progress' can so stack the cards in the competitive game that others must follow suit or lose out . . . ." J. Lintner, "Effect of Corporate Taxation on Real Investment," *American Economic Review*, Vol. XLIV, May 1954, p. 524.

have lost effective control over the organizations of which they are the legal proprietors. As has often been observed, absentee ownership increases management's reluctance to undertake risks. Reasons are not hard to find.

The remuneration of the top executive is fairly sticky. If his gamble turns out well the executive is likely to receive little permanent addition to his income stream, though profit-sharing schemes may result in his getting something out of it. Failure, on the other hand, can have serious consequences. At best, it is only embarrassing. At worst, the management group will be turned out of office.

Moreover, the executive who gambles successfully may find that his reward is worse than meager—sometimes he will suffer an indirect penalty. In fact, extraordinary but unrepeatable success may cost him almost as dear as failure. If in one year his efforts have brought in 20 percent returns, the next year he can expect to be asked why if only 12 percent was earned. As a result, businessmen may even be tempted to avoid extraordinary profits. I have been told of one large enterprise whose management realized a few weeks before the preparation of its annual report that it was likely to show spectacular profits. An energetic expenditure program (involving office modernization and other legitimate but somewhat optional purchases) was launched at once and achieved its objective—to bring the year's earnings into line and avoid spoiling the stockholders.[15]

Absentee ownership, then, means that management must curb, somewhat, its spirit of adventure because gambling comes close to being a "heads you win, tails I lose" affair. Even relatively riskless but extraordinary and temporary profit possibilities can be unattractive. It is clear that, as a result, some opportunities for innovation and expansion will be foregone. To this extent the separation of ownership from management may act as a drag on economic growth.

But just staying out of trouble will not usually keep stockholders satisfied. Management must try to keep the firm growing with little interruption. Certainly sales must not be permitted to fall or the market

[15]In objecting to the cessation of unusually high profit rates, the stockholder need not be wholly irrational. Extraordinary earnings, if the public does not know when they will cease, may be capitalized by the market on the assumption that they will continue for a substantial period. The value of the shares of the firm will rise so as to reduce relatively these earnings to a percentage rate comparable with the returns being paid out by other firms. If, subsequently, the earnings of this enterprise fall back to their previous level, the recent stock buyer will in fact have cause for complaint. He will have suffered a capital loss or, what amounts to the same thing, he will have to be content with extraordinarily low yields on the money which he has paid for the stocks.

share to decline. Expansion should be conservative and steady, and bursts of innovation and expansion are undesirable. In this, too, management in nonowner-operated firms will seek to avoid alike risk and brilliant accomplishments that raise expectations for its future conduct too high.

Therefore, when the firm in which management is separated from ownership comes across a number of expansion opportunities, if some of them can be deferred, it may pay management to keep a few of these opportunities unused and in reserve and to take advantage of them gradually. In prosperous periods this influence may even decrease total investment. On the other hand, when expansion opportunities are scarce, management may nevertheless feel itself under stockholder pressure to show some results by way of increased sales. The executive may decide, for reasons of internal politics, to expand at a modest pace even when the profitability of growth is somewhat questionable, provided only that it is not likely to be disastrous. If this happens in many firms at once, the investments can for this very reason turn out to be profitable.

In this way the separation of ownership from management can reduce the amplitude of fluctuations in investment expenditure by reducing both peaks and troughs. If all of the investment expenditure occurred during boom periods, it might, because of resource limitations, have served only to increase prices and to change the composition of investment, rather than to increase its total. Thus, this policy of constant but limited investment makes for a larger national capital stock and a greater national product.

The character of the innovation process is also affected by the separation of ownership from management. Erratic invention and discovery is no longer good enough, and research, too, must be put on a business-like basis. I believe the huge current industrial expenditures on research can partly be explained by management's demand for a dependable flow of new ideas that have been thoroughly pretested to reduce their risk to a minimum. National economic growth is thereby likely to be stimulated.

7. Concluding comment

In this chapter I have argued that the institutionalized structure and psychology of our business enterprise provides a powerful and sustained force making for the expansion of the economy. The businessman's concern with his market share, the large firm's ability to spread its risk, and the desire to promote profitability all make for expansion.

Even the conservatism that seems to result from nonowner management may serve to put expansion on a less haphazard basis and can thereby increase growth on balance. I do not maintain that these are the only expansionary influences in the economy, but I insist that an economy that lacks such forces must acquire some substitutes or find itself lagging ever further behind.

CHAPTER 11

Induced demand
for growing outputs

The discussion of the preceding chapter left one really critical gap in the argument. In examining the motives for management to expand the firm's outputs, it assumed implicitly that these incremental outputs could always somehow be marketed. Yet the source of the demand for these items is by no means obvious. In this chapter I will argue that the growth process itself is likely to generate much of the demand for the additions to output it provides. Then, in the next chapter I will consider some possible sources of demand that are exogenous to the process of expansion.

1. Demand for the increased outputs of the firm

In our model of the expanding firm it was assumed that its production increases at a constant percentage rate for the indefinite future. But the individual businessman's motivation for undertaking such a program is not entirely clear. How can he expect, year after year, to find customers for an ever-growing flow of production?

One answer is that the question implicitly applies *partial* equilibrium methods to a problem for which they are totally inappropriate. Because he will not be alone in his program of expansion, the individual seller's demand curve will not stay still as required by the partial analysis; rather, it will usually be carried upward by the general upswing. If there is simultaneous growth in the activity of a large proportion of the economy's business enterprises, incomes of employees and of suppliers of other inputs will grow commensurately, and demands for most products may be expected to shift upward.[1]

[1]This still leaves open the question of whether this shift in demand functions will be large enough to justify the increase in output. I discuss this question in the sections that follow.

But this reply only opens the way to other difficulties that arise out of the externalities problem. It can be argued that no individual producer really has any reason to grow on his own initiative beyond his stationary equilibrium output because the effect of his expansion on effective demand will largely be felt by others. The increased income of his employees and his suppliers will be devoted mostly to the purchase of other people's products. If this is so, it must pay each producer to wait for everyone else to expand. But, if everyone waits in this way, the upward movement in question will die aborning.

How can we account for the fact that things do not work out this way? First, upward movements are often initiated by what to sellers are essentially exogenous events, like increases in military expenditure, inventions, population growth, and increased foreign demand.

Second, I think a good part of the explanation lies in the fact that businessmen know so little about their cost and demand functions[2] that they have no idea whether their scale of operations is so large that further expansion will yield diminishing returns or whether they have a way to go before they will reach their equilibrium outputs. In the absence of information to the contrary, it is easy, and (because other businessmen behave similarly) even rational, to accept optimistic assumptions.

Third, businessmen in oligopolistic enterprises seem to act on the premise that promotional activity can increase sales even if all else fails. A sufficiently expensive and well-organized selling and advertising campaign is the widely accepted answer to any obstacle to growth. It is not always clear whether the resulting returns are expected to be sufficiently large to make up for the selling costs incurred or whether

[2]I have rarely encountered a businessman who asked for, or had himself obtained information about, more than single points on these functions. It was even more surprising to find how often the information management did possess was incomplete and misleading. Moreover, even businessmen who were contemplating price changes often did not think in terms of these relationships. They sometimes seemed quite willing to invent figures that assured them that these (admittedly arbitrary) price changes would work out satisfactorily. In one case a prediction of trebled sales was backed up only by vague references to trends, though in fact for a number of years there had been a pronounced and uninterrupted downward trend in the firm's sales.

This is not intended to be critical of the businessman's operations. Often, expensive research yields only fragmentary demand and cost information, and even much of that is highly questionable. Under the circumstances the decision to operate on guesswork may be making the best of a bad situation. However, the rapid growth and proliferation of consulting organizations suggest that the businessmen are themselves anxious to increase the information at their disposal and the rationality of their decisions.

the matter is just not given much thought. But in any event, the appeal of the advertising man is often irresistible to the businessman who is determined to enlarge his scale of operations. Directly or indirectly, then, the advertising man may well be justified in claiming that the product of his activity makes an important contribution to the growth of national income.

Finally, past experience has prejudiced firms to look with favor on expansion programs. When they grew in the past they often found demand waiting for them just because so many other firms were increasing their production at the same time. If every executive is convinced that the growth of his enterprise will be lucrative, the general expansion that results may turn out to have justified this belief. It is essentially a matter of faith.

These four phenomena—fortuitous expansionary events, limited entrepreneurial information on cost and demand functions, the executive's faith in advertising promotion as a remedy for mistakes, and the pleasant recollections of growth programs undertaken by him in the past—can account for the businessman's willingness to expand despite the fact that a unilateral increase in output can so easily prove disastrous.

2. Growth, induced investment, and the Harrod-Domar model

The essence of the determination of effective demand is best captured in a macroeconomic approach. First I will examine briefly the short-run consequences of an expansion in output, and then I will turn to its demand effects in the longer run.

The implication of the Harrod-Domar model[3] that is at the same time most paradoxical and most persuasive is the proposition that too slow a rate of expansion of output can be responsible for a state of overproduction. While rising outputs do of course add to supplies, they also serve to supplement demands, particularly demands for the investment goods required by the expanding levels of production. Moreover, the higher the rate of growth, the greater must be the corresponding demand for capital goods. The paradox, of course, lies in the assertion that in order to increase the rate of current utilization of capacity it is appropriate to invest, which means a raising of the level of that capacity. And the explanation is really quite simple. Growth devours savings and

[3]See, e.g., R. F. Harrod, *Toward a Dynamic Economics*, London, Macmillan, 1948; and E. D. Domar, *Essays in the Theory of Economic Growth*, New York, Oxford University Press, 1957.

thus can effectively consume the excess *ex ante* savings that depress an economy.

One does not have to accept any of the more naïve versions of the acceleration principle to believe that demand for investment will increase with dy/dt (where y is some measure of output). In fact, it is hardly plausible that it might be otherwise. But if investment demand is an increasing function of dy/dt, the Harrod-Domar conclusion follows, for, by definition, y is the volume of output supplied by the economy. Moreover, it is clearly possible to increase dy/dt today without affecting the current level of y (output may be rising rapidly whether its current level is low, middling, or high). Hence, a rise in dy/dt relative to y can increase the demand for products relative to their supply and *vice versa*. We will see presently that in one sense the increased effective demand obtained by means of a higher growth rate merely postpones the problem—a higher growth rate means higher future outputs and hence larger supplies that must somehow find a market. But it must be agreed that at a given moment of time a sufficient rate of growth should be able to wipe out excess supplies—it should constitute an effective remedy for unemployment and recession and therefore may be one of the elements of a program designed to deal with an economy operating below its capacity.[4]

3. The deflationary gap in the longer run

At this point the literature ceases to offer us guidance, and we will have to strike out on our own. To examine the longer-run demand effects of economic growth I will utilize a macroeconomic model very similar in its formal structure to the growth-equilibrium model of the firm described in the preceding chapter.

The discussion will be expressed in terms of what might be called the deflationary gap or the excess total supply, defined as total output of the economy minus desired consumption and desired investment expenditure. If the government is to carry out a successful stabilization policy, its net outlay, G, must be equal to this difference so that net government demand just suffices to take up the excess supply of national output. Thus, I will deal interchangeably with these two concepts—the excess

---

[4]It is tempting to turn the Harrod-Domar argument the other way, to assert that stimulation of output is also conducive to growth—and so it is in the short run. But in the long run, a "full-employment" policy and a growth stimulation policy are not the same thing. While a high rate of expansion can always help employment (if there is an unoccupied labor force to be had), once unemployment has been reduced to levels where the Phillips curve imposes its threat, further stimulation of demand is likely to produce inflation rather than growth.

supply of output and the requisite ("full employment") government outlay—considering the effect over time of a protracted period of growth on the values of these variables.

This viewpoint leads at once to a sort of reverse multiplier relationship that describes the level of required government expenditure as a function of national income. Let c represent the marginal propensity to consume, and let Y represent the "full-employment" income level. Then we have on the usual simple assumptions

Excess supply

= income (that is, total supply) — consumption demand — investment demand

$$E = Y - cY - I$$

so that if the government is to make up for this excess by its expenditure ($G = E$) we obtain $dG/dY = 1 - c$. For obvious reasons, then, the increase in government expenditure called for by a given rise in output is given by $(1 - c)$, the inverse of the usual multiplier.

This, however, tells us only about the effect of a once and for all increase in Y. Even with full employment, some rate of increase in output, g, is made possible by capital accumulation, a growing labor force, and changes in technology, and it is possible to conceive of policy measures that would stimulate a rise in g. If the rise in growth rate is permanent, all future incomes will be affected, and the need for government outlays will be increased through the workings of the inverse multiplier. But the increase in growth rate also will have another consequence. As we have seen from our brief discussion of the Harrod-Domar analysis, it will induce an offsetting increase in investment demand. Our earlier discussion might then appear to suggest that the net consequence will be a decrease in the required expenditure of the government.

But that is a short-sighted conclusion, for a higher growth rate today produces higher incomes tomorrow, and while the one reduces the over-all level of excess supply, the other increases it. Where, then, do we come out on balance? I shall show now that if the usual oversimplified assumptions hold, then as a result of more rapid growth the real government outlays required to eliminate excess supplies ultimately will be increased in absolute terms (indeed, they will continue to increase with the passage of time). However, their magnitude will necessarily fall relative to the size of the real national income.

To show this I assume again that the (permanent) rate of growth of full employment output is g. Then G_t, the required government outlay in period t, is given by desired savings minus desired investment in that period, that is, by

(11.1) $G_t = (1 - c)Y_t - k \Delta Y_t.$

Here $k \Delta Y_t$ equals net investment in period t so that investment is determined in accord with the simplest form of the acceleration principle and is strictly proportionate to the absolute rate of growth of income.[5] We have for the undiscounted value of income $Y_t = (1 + g)^t Y_0$ so that

$$\Delta Y_t = Y_{t+1} - Y_t = (1 + g)^t Y_0 (1 + g - 1)$$
$$= g(1 + g)^t Y_0.$$

Substituting into (11.1) we have

(11.2) $G_t = Y_0 (1 - c - kg)(1 + g)^t.$

Hence, differentiating with respect to g,

$$\frac{dG_t}{dg} = Y_0 t (1 + g)^{t-1} (1 - c - kg) - Y_0 k (1 + g)^t,$$

or writing $Y_t = Y_0 (1 + g)^t$, this derivative equals

$$Y_{t-1}[t(1 - c - kg) - k(1 + g)],$$

which is positive if t is sufficiently large and grows without limit with t, because, by (11.2), for any values of g that are plausible economically and politically $(1 - c - kg) > 0$ (otherwise government expenditures would have to be nonpositive). In other words, a growth stimulation policy (with full employment) must eventually (but perhaps only after a *very* long interval) increase the real resources available to government and increase them more and more with the passage of time despite the fact that it also stimulates the use of resources for private investment.[6]

[5]It would be illegitimate in terms of the logic of the acceleration principle to adopt an investment demand function of the form $I = kg$ which would have *absolute* investment proportionate to the *percentage* rate of growth. This would imply that a huge economy and a tiny economy both require the same number of new factories to expand their outputs by 5 percent, an assumption that is obviously nonsense.

[6]The net effect in terms of present value is ambiguous, however. Let r be the discount rate where, for the usual reasons, we take $r > g$ (see Ch. 10, fn. 5). Then, by (11.2) the discounted present value of the infinite(?) stream of G_t is

$$G = Y_0 (1 - c - kg)(1 + r)/(r - g),$$

for which

$$dG/dg = (1 - c - kr)Y_0 (1 + r)/(r - g)^2$$

whose sign will be positive if and only if $(1 - c - kr) > 0$, whereas all the information we have is $(1 - c - kg) > 0$ and $r > g$.

However, in this model a rise in g will always *decrease* governmental resources *as a proportion of full employment income*, for by (11.2)

$$\frac{G_t}{Y_t} = 1 - c - kg,$$

which will always fall as g increases.

Of course, these conclusions are no more persuasive than the highly oversimplified model from which they are derived. But they do suggest that the Harrod-Domar proposition utilized in the preceding section does require some little qualification. While more rapid growth will in the first instance reduce any deflationary gap, in the very long run, by increasing the crescendo of the stream of outputs, it may well cause the absolute size of that gap to rise, though the gap may be expected to fall as a proportion of total output. Yet the over-all tenor of the result is reassuring. It does suggest that the process of growth is likely to provide a substantial proportion of its required demand. Thus, we have arrived at a sort of dynamized Say's Law; modified and qualified though it may be, it can be rather comforting. While more quickly growing outputs may require ever larger increases in government outlays to maintain full employment, if as a result of more rapid growth those outlays fall as a proportion of total national income, the burden of stabilization policy will certainly not be made heavier.

4. Corollary: growth and the availability of public services

This discussion has incidental implications about some alleged benefits of a growth stimulation program that are worth considering briefly. It has been suggested that in some of the more affluent economies more rapid growth is desirable not primarily as an end in itself but because of its felicitous side effects. Closer examination reveals, however, that these consequences are not always as certain as they may seem at first. For example, it has been suggested more than once that more rapid expansion can be helpful to a nation experiencing balance of payments difficulties. Yet a little thought indicates that growth may sometimes aggravate the problem. By causing a rise in prices, growth may discourage exports, and its input requirements and the higher incomes it provides to the members of the economy may both produce a substantial rise in imports.

A growth policy has sometimes been advocated also as a means of providing the resources for increased supplies of public goods and social services. Professor Galbraith has forcefully argued that there has been a substantial lag in the provision of public services relative to the increasing affluence of our society.[7] Even if one does not agree that the consumer's ability to make effective use of a growing abundance declines sharply at the margin, most of us will surely acquiesce in the view that much remains to be done through the agency of the public sector. The deterioration of our cities, the pressing demands of our educational systems, and the persistence of poverty all pose problems that bear critically upon the quality of living in the society of the future. In our dealings with some of these difficulties we have made little visible progress—in some cases we may even be receding from our goals.

That being the case, there is good ground for concern with the magnitude of the real resources that governments have available to them to deal with these issues. And it has been suggested that one of the benefits of more rapid economic growth is the increased flow of wealth that it places at the disposal of the public sector. In one obvious sense this conclusion is indisputable. Tax systems are usually structured in such a way that expanding incomes automatically produce larger tax yields, and if taxes are progressive, these yields may grow not only absolutely, but also as a proportion of national income.

Yet this is not the main issue. Tax regulations are made by man and are subject to change. In any event, surely the appropriate measure of the resources available to the government is the amount it can spend without serious inflationary consequences. Thus, the excess supply variable in our model of the preceding section becomes the relevant consideration, and G, the net government outlay that is consistent with economic stability, is the pertinent index of the resources at the disposition of the public sector without great political strain.

But our model suggests, then, that taken over-all, increased growth may constitute a rather mixed blessing from the point of view of the provision of public services. It indicates that increased output will *ultimately* raise G_t—it will ultimately put more resources at the disposal of public bodies. But that may only occur in the very distant future, and the immediate effect of faster growth is likely to be such a rise in investment demand that governments will have to cut down their spending if inflationary consequences are to be avoided. Even in the long run, more rapid growth, while it will offer more extensive resources for public purposes, may cause total output to grow even more rapidly so that, relatively speaking, it may generate political pressures that force government outlays to fall further and further behind.

[7]See J. K. Galbraith, *The Affluent Society*, Boston, Houghton Mifflin, 1958.

Thus, while growth is a desirable end in itself, and in advanced economies it may be wanted as a means to provide military security[8] and as a way to help attain other noneconomic ends, there is no guarantee that it can serve very effectively in the promotion of a number of economic objectives for which it has sometimes been prescribed. Thus, in our more advanced economies, society will have to decide largely on noneconomic grounds and on the merits of growth itself whether it is willing to pay the high price required to institute a substantial and sustained growth stimulation program.

[8]However, if increased growth does not effectively add to the resources at the disposal of the government it may actually make it harder for a democratic state to build up its military strength. This represents a modification in some views I expressed earlier. See K. Knorr and W. Baumol, eds., *What Price Economic Growth?* Englewood Cliffs, Prentice-Hall, 1961, especially Appendix A.

CHAPTER 12

Autonomous demand for growing outputs

Powerful though they may be, all of the expansionary influences I have discussed can obviously be frustrated by a shortage of demand. Indeed, the stagnation thesis has asserted that the rapid growth of the American economy is approaching its end because willingness to purchase is not keeping up with outputs. I am not inclined to accept this view, which has, I believe, been colored excessively by the unhappy experience of the 1930's. From a long-run point of view, Haavelmo's characterization of depressions as so-called " 'catastrophes' of ten per cent dents in ... national income" comes much closer to the truth. Certainly the view that business expansion itself, more often than not, will produce a demand for its increased output seems to be supported by the history of national incomes in modern capitalist economies.[1]

1. Induced investment: short run

On the other side, a literal reading of the Keynesian income analysis may lead us to doubt that even widespread increases in supply will be able to create their own demand.[2] Granted that a general expansion will produce some increase in incomes and hence, in demand, there

[1]But recently, P. M. Sweezy has called attention to Veblen's contrary view, "that since the 1870's 'chronic depression has been the rule rather than the exception in business.' " *Cf.* P. M. Sweezy, "Professor Cole's History of Socialist Thought," *American Economic Review*, Vol. XLVII, December 1957, and T. Veblen, *The Theory of Business Enterprise*, New York, Scribners, 1904, especially Ch. 7.

[2]This view, that production creates the income with which goods can be bought is, incidentally, one of the several somewhat contradictory versions of Say's Law that can be read into Say's writings. See J. B. Say, *A Treatise on Political Economy*, Prinsep, trans., Philadelphia, Lippincott, 1852, pp. 136–37, and his *Oeuvres Diverses*, Paris, 1848, p. 441.

remains the question whether this induced upward shift in the demand functions, by itself, will be adequate to permit profitable sales of all the increased outputs that brought it about. The Keynesian analysis suggests that, after some point, demand will fail to keep up with production. Because the marginal propensity to consume is less than unity, a rise in output above its Keynesian equilibrium level will bring *ex ante* savings above the more or less stationary level of investment demand, and so demand will prove inadequate to take up the increased national product. But an expansionary movement itself will produce a fairly steady rise in the Keynesian equilibrium income level by shifting upward the investment demand. It is another case of investment that produces a demand for further investment.

Indeed, the standard rules of thumb may result in a rise in investment demand roughly proportional with any increase in output. For if, in the absence of any alarming portents, firms allocate a fixed proportion of their increased gross sales revenues to investment (as I believe is often the case in practice), such an increase in investment demand may well result.

A rise in consumption demand proportionate with any increase in output is also not unlikely, even in the short run, as both the empirical evidence and the Duesenberry argument indicate.[3] But if investment and consumption demand can both increase in proportion with output, then, if governmental and export demands do not fall behind, effective demand can keep up with any production rise that results from expansionary business goals.

In any event, some increase in investment can always be expected as a concomitant of rising output. In addition, the accompanying increases in selling expenditures and the optimism that frequently results from rising incomes can be expected to tend to raise consumption functions.[4] For these reasons business growth plans may be expected to work out well more often than not. Of course there is always the possibility that an upward movement in output will not call forth enough of an increase in demand to sustain itself, and that can lead to a crisis. But I have argued that, even in the short run, this is neither the necessary nor even the normal result of the businessman's efforts to expand. In the next section I suggest that over long periods the problem of effective demand may be even less serious.

[3] *Income, Saving, and the Theory of Consumer Behavior*, Cambridge, Mass., Harvard University Press, 1949, pp. 32–37.

[4] Though there will be offsetting influences as well, e.g., rising investment will tend to increase interest rates.

2. Long-run determinants of investment

In the long run I believe that investment demand constitutes no important source of difficulty for business expansion. The desire to increase their incomes and to accumulate wealth, in the long run, will lead people to keep their investment demand as high as they can manage. As a result, changes in the rate of profit have very little effect on the motive for accumulation,[5] and investment demand may well continue high so long as it yields any positive returns, however small. I do not wish to disguise the fact that this is largely an unsupported allegation.

As I shall argue in Chapter 13, a good many of the objectives men pursue require wealth for their attainment, and wealth is usually attractive in and of itself. It therefore is difficult to believe that there will ever be a long period when those in a position to do so are not willing to accumulate wealth on the most favorable terms available. Any positive rate of return on investment is precisely that—an added opportunity to accumulate. The most promising investment opportunity at any time offers the most favorable terms available to those who obtain income by letting their wealth earn for them.

Willingness to invest on whatever terms are available must be increased by the invidious aspects of accumulation—the desire to be wealthier than someone else, rather than just to be wealthy. Those who join this race can afford to neglect no opportunity to increase their accumulation rate. He who fails to invest when the rate of return is positive is offering to others the opportunity to catch up with, or to get ahead of, him. Moreover, low returns can act as less of a deterrent to the potential investor whose primary concern is his relative position, because others are likely to be doing no better.

I would suggest, then, that investment is geared to the level of income through the propensity to save, rather than to profit rates. The desire to acquire wealth puts the individual under pressure to invest, in the long run, almost everything he saves and, except when expectations are peculiarly unfavorable, to add little to his idle balances.[6]

[5]It must be admitted, however, that the level of profit rates may have a substantial indirect effect on investment. By changing the distribution of income it can affect the volume of savings in the manner which has so often been discussed. Low profit rates, by reducing the incomes of the wealthy, may reduce their savings, not because they want to accumulate less but because they have less to save.

[6]On the other hand, very low cash balances also can be costly, but optimally cash balances can be expected to increase less than in proportion with transactions. See my "The Transactions Demand for Cash: An Inventory Theoretic Approach," *Quarterly Journal of Economics*, Vol. LXVI, November 1952, and J. Tobin, "The Interest-Elasticity of Transactions Demand for Cash," *Review of Economics and Statistics*, Vol. XXXVIII, August 1956.

I believe, then, that the developed economies are essentially Schumpeterian worlds where the drive for wealth (and through it the drive to innovate) in the long run keeps up the demand for investment and thereby the demand for consumption and still further investment. Investment creates the prosperity that justifies the investment. This is why I believe that for longer run problems it is appropriate to consider saving as a source of productive accumulation rather than as a deterrent to it.[7] I much prefer this reason for rejecting the stagnation thesis to the set of arguments associated with the wealth-saving relationship,[8] though there is no necessary conflict between the two views.

I think that to some extent my investment hypothesis applies also to underdeveloped areas. Even in this case we may usually expect to find unused opportunities to invest savings profitably because incomes and hence savings are ordinarily so low that savings may be expected to fall short of the available investment opportunities.[9] Furthermore, for reasons given in the next chapter, I believe that even in underdeveloped regions the wealthy will want to take advantage of profitable investment opportunities. Unfortunately, many of the investments they do undertake are of a sort that adds little to the economy's productive capacity.

3. Comments

The reader perhaps has been struck by the largely impressionistic basis of the optimistic conclusions of this chapter. The view that prosperity, rather than depression, is the normal long-run state of our economy is, after all, merely an amateur piece of social psychologizing that asserts that entrepreneurs will tend, in the long run, to be sufficiently buoyant to demand for investment all that the public wishes to save, and perhaps even more.

But one cannot easily dismiss the suspicion that such views are born most frequently in a period of almost uninterrupted expansion and inflation, just as the stagnation thesis may have been a child of the great

[7]Investment can sometimes be profitable but socially unproductive. In the next chapter I suggest that this may be a particularly serious problem for the underdeveloped areas.

[8]For a discussion of this application of the relationship, see G. Haberler, "The Pigou Effect Once More," *Journal of Political Economy*, Vol. LX, June 1952.

[9]This was Keynes' position. See *The General Theory of Employment, Interest, and Money*, New York, Harcourt, Brace & World, 1936, pp. 31, 219–20. But it reasonably can be asked whether in some undeveloped areas incomes and savings are low *just because* investment opportunities are poor. Certainly this crucial question merits further empirical investigation because an area in which there are few profitable investment opportunities may well be "undevelopable."

depression. It is all too easy to extrapolate our brief, most recent experience and elevate it into a major historical tendency.[10]

Even the fact that our economic history has been expansionary over so long a period is far from conclusive. Can this not, to a considerable extent, have been the product of a sequence of events, which as far as the economic mechanism is concerned, were largely fortuitous? The inventions, the growth of population, and even the diplomatic and military events that gave such impetus to growth and helped so much to sustain effective demand were doubtless all influenced by economic happenings but, surely, by other things as well. Today, also, one may well ask whether in the absence of the cold war and its unprecedented levels of military expenditures the postwar expansion would have continued as long as it did.

These questions cannot be dismissed lightly. I can only repeat that my impressions of the nature of business motivations lead me to feel that in this respect things do work out well in the long run, and that left to itself the economy will continue to expand, though not without serious interruptions.

4. The long-run investment hypothesis and the acceleration principle

In the course of the argument of this chapter I have put forth the hypothesis that in the long run investment will be influenced more by the level of income than by the rate of profit. In this and the next section I digress to discuss the relationship between the acceleration principle and my hypothesis, as well as one of its implications.

It should be noted first that my hypothesis is clearly not an acceleration principle relationship. It asserts that investment will vary directly with the level, rather than the rate of change, of income. It must be remembered, however, that this is asserted for the long run and not necessarily for the short run.[11] My reason is straightforward enough. Because I believe that in the long run the public will invest as much as it

[10]But note the following statement, which appeared in 1938! "It may be . . . that in this country we are still habituated to the belief that the normal expectancy for most enterprises is growth and expansion accompanied by increasing profitability. . . . Yet [despite recent experience] the association of growth with increasing profitability may be so much a part of our historical experience that many business executives are still acting as if it ought to be realized in most enterprises." N. S. Buchanan, "Theory and Practice in Dividend Distribution," *Quarterly Journal of Economics*, Vol. LIII, November 1938, p. 83.

[11]This is precisely the reverse of Mr. Kaldor's position. See "A Model of Economic Growth," *Economic Journal*, Vol. LXVII, December 1957. I may remark that his long-run acceleration principle assumption certainly seems a questionable device for

can, its investment will after all be determined by the volume of saving, which, in turn, appears to depend heavily on output levels. The logic of the acceleration principle, on the other hand, is that as output expands, capital equipment must keep pace. Certainly, whatever validity it may have in the short run, the assertion is very doubtful in a long-run context when changes in technology are to be expected that can affect capital-output ratios radically. Long-run analysis must take account of possible technological change not only because the passage of time brings new inventions, but also because the long run permits the redesign of capital equipment in accord with inventions that were already known but which only larger scale rendered economically feasible. In the short run an increase in output may call for the introduction of more machines of the variety currently employed. But as the firm's equipment wears out or becomes obsolete it may pay to introduce capital of an entirely different nature, and we are left with little ground to assume in advance that the capital-output ratio will remain constant as the acceleration principle requires.

In contrast with its relation to the acceleration principle, there is no necessary conflict between my investment hypothesis and the time preference analysis. As so many writers since Cassel have pointed out, a fall in profit rates has an income as well as a substitution effect. It makes profit earners poorer unless they can raise enough additional capital to make up for the fall in the rate of return. Thus, like Keynes, we may argue that it is by no means clear that a fall in the rate of profit will reduce saving by very much, if it does so at all.[12]

---

arguing that the apparent constancy of capital-output ratios is no historical accident. After all, the acceleration principle *asserts* that capital-output ratios will be constant, so that in this premise he appears, in effect, to have assumed what he sets out to prove.

[12]It is worth noting, incidentally, that any statistical test of my hypothesis must run into a problem that has plagued econometricians elsewhere. Even if the data were to indicate that a sharp drop in interest and profit rates can lead to a large fall in the rate of investment, one would have to be careful to distinguish impact effects from long-run relationships. I do not doubt that a sudden departure from accustomed rates of return may lead to immediate resentment and a feeling that saving is no longer worthwhile. My contention is only that after a while people will become habituated to the new profit levels and the drive for such wealth as can be had will eventually reconcile investors to them. I suspect that failure to separate impact effects from more lasting consequences has led observers to exaggerated impressions of the values of other elasticities as well. In other words, I am suggesting that, contrary to the more usual view, many psychological-economic relationships are *more* elastic in the short run than they are in the long run. For some evidence that seems to point in this direction, see S. E. Rolfe and G. Furness, "The Impact of Changes in Tax Rates and Method of Collection on Effort: Some Empirical Observations," *Review of Economics and Statistics*, Vol. XXXIX, November 1957.

5. The investment hypothesis and the classical stationary state

If my investment hypothesis is valid, it destroys much of the basis of the classical stationary state argument that rests on the belief that some sufficiently small (positive) rate of profit will reduce net saving to zero.[13] So long as there is any return to investment, on my hypothesis, investment will continue and the "progressive state" will not disappear. Only if every useful investment opportunity has been exhausted, so that an economy is overdeveloped in the most extreme sense of the word, can the built-in impetus toward further movement cease.[14] Of course there then really would be no justification for further net investment.

In fact, few if any economies today are even approximately stationary. Total output is growing almost everywhere, perhaps largely as a result of the diffusion of technological knowledge from the more rapidly growing economies. Even in underdeveloped countries like India, production seems to be growing at a rate that has permitted very large increases in population, presumably with no marked reduction in living standards, such as they are.[15]

6. Conclusion: implications for underdeveloped areas

In the two preceding chapters we have examined the growth mechanism that characterizes the Western capitalist economies. We have seen that these societies provide strong pressures that drive continually for increased output. This suggests that, unless parallel pressures can be

[13]See, e.g., David Ricardo, "On the Principles of Political Economy and Taxation" in *The Works and Correspondence of David Ricardo*, P. Sraffa, ed., Vol. I, Cambridge, Cambridge University Press, 1951, p. 290. For a more extended discussion, see Book IV of any late edition of J. S. Mill's *Principles of Political Economy.*

[14]If with diminishing returns and population growth, the rate of profit were to approach zero asymptotically, accumulation would on my hypothesis never stop, because profits would never disappear entirely. *Cf.* W. Fellner, *Trends and Cycles in Economic Activity*, New York, Holt, Rinehart & Winston, 1956, pp. 200–203.

[15]Of course, this has resulted, at least in part, from what Fellner has called "offsets to diminishing returns" (*ibid.,* Ch. 8).

Note, however, that this last paragraph involves an inconsistency on my part. In Ch. 9, I proposed to use per capita income as my index of growth. In this sense, there is some doubt whether the Indian economy has grown at all. Rather, it may be in a state of what Professor Leibenstein has called "quasi-stability," so that there is no necessary inconsistency between the position I have taken here and Leibenstein's view that at least some of the underdeveloped areas are in a state of low-level equilibrium. See his *Economic Backwardness and Economic Growth*, New York, John Wiley, 1957, pp. 18ff and 102.

introduced into the underdeveloped areas, then (what with the other handicaps under which they find themselves) they can only expect to find themselves falling further and further behind.

But the prospects for a program to bring these Western capitalist growth forces to bear on the underdeveloped economies are not encouraging. The expansionary forces that have been called to our attention by Schumpeter and those which were discussed in the preceding chapter are all dependent on the structure of the economy's business enterprises and the attitudes and goals of its entrepreneurs. The drive to innovate, the choice of growth and market share as business goals, the competitive advantage of larger firms, and the routinization of research and other expansionary activities fostered by separation of ownership from management are all of this variety. I think it is hardly necessary to argue that none of these can be introduced overnight, if they can be introduced artificially at all. The development planner may well conclude that the Western experience provides him with standards against which he must measure up, but that for at least some portions of his program he must seek inspiration elsewhere. I shall return to a discussion of these alternative approaches to development policy in the last two chapters of this book.

CHAPTER 13

Accumulation without socially productive asset creation

Having discussed some of the forces that make for rapid economic development in the modern capitalist economies, I turn now to an examination of several features of the investment mechanism in some other economies that have slowed down their rates of growth. In this chapter I put forward two basic contentions: first, that in most under-developed economies there are to be found men interested in the pursuit or preservation of their wealth and, second, that in such economies the drive for wealth has typically not been as effectively channeled into increasing productivity as it has in the areas in which economic growth is rapid.

1. Accumulation of consumers' durables

It is not unusual to find the unproductive use of savings listed as a serious problem for the underdeveloped areas.[1] In many places savings are difficult enough to come by because of the extreme poverty of so large a proportion of the inhabitants. If such saving as can reasonably be hoped for is to be of much help in raising living standards, it must be used to create productive equipment or to improve existing facilities, for example, by technical training for the labor force. However, as writers in this field frequently point out, the wealthy sometimes choose instead to acquire palaces, hunting parks, and other luxuries.[2] Governments, too, often indulge in palace and monument building—examples are obvious enough. The scale of some of these expenditures has been so

---

[1] E.g., N. S. Buchanan and H. S. Ellis, *Approaches to Economic Development*, New York, Twentieth Century Fund, 1955, p. 521, and J. Viner, *International Trade and Economic Development*, Glencoe, The Free Press, 1952, p. 106.

[2] See, e.g., W. A. Lewis, *The Theory of Economic Growth*, Homewood, Illinois, Irwin, 1955, p. 28.

large that the nation's public finance and even the entire economy has been affected.

No one can deny that failure to turn accumulated savings into productive assets can be costly. But I shall argue in this chapter that investment in such consumer durables is not the only or even always the most important source of that difficulty. This is no mere quibble, for my hypotheses and the consumer durables view may call for the use of rather different methods to increase productive employment of accumulated savings.

2. Private versus socially productive asset accumulation

In many, if not in most, societies, wealth is helpful and even requisite for the attainment of power, prestige, or other widely held goals, and whether it is desired as a means to other ends or as an end in itself, it is plausible that wealth will be sought after even in societies unlike our own.[3] But wealth acquisition, like any activity, requires its tools and equipment. That is to say, the effective pursuit of wealth requires investment in assets that yield returns to their owners. Palaces and hunting grounds are not designed primarily for this purpose. A hypothesis that the wealthy in some societies will purchase little but consumer goods must impute to them a sort of suicidal behavior. By doing nothing to replenish the wealth they pour into these projects, they soon are likely to become impoverished. Instances of this sort of improvident behavior, of course, can be found,[4] but it is difficult to believe that it afflicts whole societies with any degree of frequency. Moreover, such a view should lead us to expect considerably greater turnover in the wealthy classes than casual observation suggests to be the case.[5]

More generally, it is my belief that economic motivations play a much more important role in relatively primitive economies than is often supposed. There is an extensive anthropological literature on this point in which opinion is somewhat divided, but there is an impressive group

[3]*Cf.* W. A. Lewis, *ibid.*, pp. 26–29.

[4]Even here we must be prepared to distinguish between intentions and failure to carry them out successfully. For example, Thomas Jefferson quite consistently managed to spend more than his income, and Monticello, his "palace building," apparently accounted for a significant part of this deficit. But he always intended to work his way out of this unhappy situation. The various schemes hatched by his fertile mind included the setting up of a not entirely successful nail factory and various plans for rationalizing the agricultural activities on his plantation.

[5]Although continued demand for durable consumer assets may cause a secular inflation in their values that maintains, or even increases, the wealth of their owners. *Cf.* Sec. 3, below.

of writers that inclines to the view to which I subscribe.[6] At a minimum, the individuals can be depended on to want somewhat more than the income that offers them the means for minimum subsistence. In such a case harder work can be elicited by a system of penalties that deprives them of this little income unless they increase their efforts. We are told that in colonial areas laborers have been obtained quite effectively from among primitive peoples by levying a tax, funds for whose payment could only be acquired by working for the foreigner.[7] Moreover, most practical development problems do not arise in regions that are largely inhabited by primitive peoples. I believe the resident of the kind of area that seeks to expand usually wants higher earnings,[8] although his drive for increased income may well be considerably weaker than that of a representative American in a closely corresponding economic position.

I base this view partly on the experience of several American firms that export to such countries. These firms have found that incentive compensation plans for their native sales forces have, at least in urban areas, often achieved a spectacular increase in sales, a result difficult to reconcile with the hypothesis that the residents of those areas are entirely uninterested in the magnitude of their earnings.

In sum, I believe that in most economies there are people who behave in some respects like economic men. In particular, I am convinced that the wealthy in most economies are prepared to save and to invest in order to maintain their wealth. How, then, does the investment process fail to contribute to the growth of the underdeveloped areas as effectively as it does to ours? I think much of the answer is that often even

[6]"Not the rashest proponent of the theory of native insensibility to monetary inducement has said that given the opportunity the natives cannot spend money. What is claimed is that they will not earn it. . . . In fact, what is condemned as laziness or dislike of work on the part of the native has often been in essentials a reluctance to expend a large amount of effort upon inefficient and poorly remunerated forms of labor." I. C. Greaves, *Modern Production Among Backward Peoples*, London, Allen and Unwin, 1935, pp. 162–63 as quoted in W. Moore, *Industrialization and Labor*, Ithaca, Cornell University Press, 1951, pp. 83–84. Though he seems to agree, Moore also cites some contrary evidence (pp. 21–44). See also, e.g., C. S. Belshaw, *In Search of Wealth*, American Anthropological Association Memoir No. 80, Menasha, Wisconsin, 1955, especially pp. 37, 41, and 63.

[7]See W. Moore, *op. cit.*, pp. 67–69.

[8]"The situation with respect to direct monetary incentives is clearly somewhat different in old, peasant civilizations where some degree of monetary exchange has long been built into customary practices. There the potential industial worker is likely to require no sweeping change of attitude in order to be interested in wages as such, although the sacrifices entailed in a shift of occupation may be such that a minor monetary advantage will not be sufficient inducement in the absence of various pressures 'from behind.' " W. Moore, *op. cit.*, p. 84.

the profitable investments undertaken in such areas are of a sort that add little or nothing to the productive capacity of the economy.[9] Some of these investments can be even worse than that, as we shall see.

3. Investment in land and other previously existing assets

As a first example of the channeling of the pursuit of wealth into unproductive outlets, let us consider landholding. The analysis applies equally to the holding of other income-yielding assets whose production is not increased by their purchase—for example, the buying of previously issued corporate stocks. Keynes has called our attention to the importance of landholding as an unproductive form of investment.[10] Keynes' meaning is not entirely clear, but for our purposes it is sufficient to note that landholding pure and simple (as opposed to landholding *and* improvement), has at various times been, and in some areas still is, a fairly popular form of investment.[11] The importance of the distinction cannot be exaggerated. The landholder who takes pride in the effectiveness of the agricultural methods employed on his land, who is continually investing in fertilizers, better plant strains, and equipment, and who is anxious to innovate is indeed promoting national productivity. It is equally obvious that this is not true of the man who does little but hold title to his land. Yet landholding of the latter variety may be lucrative enough and has the additional attraction of requiring little time and effort of a sort that is even considered reprehensible in some societies.

As has been pointed out,[12] the social waste involved in investment in existing assets is more subtle than it may at first appear. Unlike palace

[9]For a very good statement of the distinction between profitable and productive investments see R. Solo, "The Accumulation of Wealth in the Form of Land Ownership in Underdeveloped Areas," *Land Economics*, Vol. XXXI, May 1955.

[10]*The General Theory of Employment, Interest, and Money*, New York, Harcourt, Brace & World, 1936, pp. 241–42. See also Solo, *op. cit.*

[11]Professor Viner, *loc. cit.*, has questioned both the meaning and the general validity of the Keynesian proposition, pointing out that at some times, and in some places, landholders were "improving" landlords and arguing that they might, in fact, have been making the most productive investments possible from the point of view of the national economy. These strictures are not relevant to my present point because I am neither questioning the productivity of agricultural capital goods nor maintaining that the sort of landholder I am describing is a ubiquitous phenomenon. But to suggest that he sometimes exists, it may be enough to contrast the worst of the nineteenth-century Irish landlords with Viner's eighteenth-century English and Scottish landholders.

[12]See Solo, *op. cit.* and H. Leibenstein, *Economic Backwardness and Economic Growth*, New York, John Wiley, 1957, pp. 117–19.

building, it does not directly use up any of society's real resources. Speculative land purchases, security purchases, and the buying of other existing assets only transfer liquid assets from one owner to another. But an important social cost is involved in the loss of an opportunity to direct resources from consumption to productive asset creation. The owners of assets whose value is increased will be induced to spend more on consumers' goods that are produced domestically or are imported with scarce foreign currency. Perhaps even more serious is the tremendous waste of entrepreneurial talent devoted to the effective operation of such ventures. A network of middlemen, administrators, etc., may be expected to arise in response to the demand for their services, and much of the community's business ability may be absorbed into activities that result in no more than the transfer of goods.

This type of investment, while socially unproductive, can increase the investor's wealth in two ways—through the collection of rent and through capital gains. The latter may require some comment because, by hypothesis, this landholder makes no "real" additions to his holdings. But so long as the supply of land is limited and the wealthy continue to seek to purchase it with their incomes, the price of land (and perhaps sometimes of its products) may be expected to rise. This secular inflation in land values yields the capital gains that bring forth the investment that produces it. It also means that there need never be a shortage of land to meet the demands of those who seek new investment outlets for their accumulations. The inflationary process can expand the supply without limit.

The net effect, if sellers of land use their sale proceeds to buy other land, however, is merely to redistribute the wealth of the economy rather than add to it. The inflation increases the wealth of old landholders at the expense of new landholders or other members of the community.[13]

As I have already stated, these remarks need not be confined to landholding. They apply equally where the purchase of any previously

---

[13]This may be limited, as can be the redistributive consequences of any inflation, by the price responsiveness of related items, e.g., money wages (but not real wages) may be pushed up by the demand for labor to cultivate the increasingly valuable agricultural properties and by any reduction in population that results from increased impoverishment of the lower income groups. But such forces can usually be expected to serve as no more than partial offsets to the redistributional effect of the inflation of land values, for these countervailing price movements are ordinarily produced only by substantial changes in relative values and in the relative economic well-being of the members of the economy; i.e., the offsets cannot completely eliminate the redistribution that brings them about, for they would disappear long before the redistributive effect was eliminated completely.

existing asset is considered the most prudent form of investment, as when gold or jewels are bought, at least partly, for financial purposes. For this reason I should not be surprised if the analysis was found to be relevant to a significant proportion of the investment undertaken in underdeveloped areas.

4. Investment in martial equipment

Let us examine another case where economic growth can be argued to have been retarded not by lack of economic interest but by its misdirection. Historically the support and equipment of private armies has been a very important form of investment. It is still occasionally encountered as the main economic activity of war lords or local rulers of politically fragmentized areas, but above all, it was a basic feature of the feudal economy. The contention that some light can be shed on the behavior of medieval barons by considering them as economic men may seem rather farfetched, but the facts seem almost to demand this interpretation.[14] For example, the self-seeking behavior of the powerful nobles during the Anarchy, the period when Stephen and Matilda were battling for the English Crown, was easily as blatant as that of Adam Smith's merchant who rarely "affected to trade for the public good." Perhaps only in the story of Jay Gould and some of his associates can any modern parallel be found. Among the most enterprising of these barons was Geoffrey de Mandeville, that earlier kingmaker, whose tergiversations from contender to contender (each time exhorting more lands and privileges as the price of his brief partnership) cry out for a game theoretic analysis.[15] Much of the soldiering of the Hundred Years' War, to give another example, seems to have had an economic inspiration, having been carried out with an eye to lands and booty.

I must not give the impression of contending that the amassing of wealth for its own sake was an important objective of the medieval

[14]Actually, the economy of the later Middle Ages exhibits other surprising similarities with more recent periods; e.g., there were many self-made men or men who rose from the ranks. Among the best known of these are Hubert Walter, Richard the Lion Hearted's wealthy and powerful Archbishop of Canterbury and Judiciar, William Marshal, regent of England during the minority of Henry III, and Thomas à Becket. Royal policy sometimes involved promotion of upstarts as an offset to the power of the nobility. This often led to trouble, as in the case of the baronial protests against Richard II's appointees. At times it also backfired when, as in the case of St. Thomas, the king's creature became too powerful and turned against his master.

[15]The reader may be interested to know that Earl Geoffrey finally came out on the short end of his payoff function. He was killed after a final period during which he was a hunted, excommunicated marauder.

nobility. It is really as pointless to argue this as to discuss the parallel generalization about modern businessmen. No doubt a plausible case can be made for the view that the members of the Morgan dynasty were more interested in power than in money, and the same, perhaps, may be surmised about some designers of elaborate holding company structures. Nor does my case rest on the necessarily few and miscellaneous illustrations that can be cited in this sort of discussion. I readily admit that the typical goal of the feudal magnate was some undefinable complex compounded of position, glory, power, wealth, and many other elements.[16] To some extent, their behavior may merely have been the result of pressure toward conformity.

But whatever may have been the barons' goals, and these undoubtedly varied from case to case, it took wealth to achieve them. It seems to me there can be little doubt that this wealth was frequently sought, more or less systematically, as a means if not as an end.[17] On this score, the record of the royal household is clear. The struggle for financial support from the country is one of the central themes of the political history of medieval England. Such important items as the Domesday Book and the origins and development of Parliament are directly connected with the public finances. Thus, slow economic growth in the Middle Ages cannot be ascribed to complete lack of economic interest on the part of the wealthy and powerful.

Moreover, the discussion suggests that in many cases the medieval quest for wealth took the form of military ventures. In the case of the king this was often fairly clearly the case,[18] and for the subject, plunder

[16]"In his youth a man should use without laziness or delay, his prowess, his valor, and the vigor of his body for the honor and profit of himself and his dependents. . . . The young nobleman, knight, or man-at-arms should work to acquire honor, to be renowned for valor, and to have temporal possessions, riches, and heritages on which he can live honorably." Philippe de Navarre, *Les Quatre Ages de l'Homme* (thirteenth century), ed., M. de Fréville, Société des Anciens Textes Français, 1888, pp. 38–39, quoted in S. Painter, *William Marshal*, Baltimore, Johns Hopkins Press, 1933, p. 30.

[17]See the charming account of William Marshal's first lesson in warfare as an economic enterprise in Painter, *ibid.*, p. 22. He must have learned his lesson well. Largely by his own effort he rose from an insecure position as the fourth son of a minor English baron to become one of the wealthiest men in England.

[18]Perhaps the most obviously economic military policy was that of Henry VII who, like Edward IV before him, arranged to be paid handsomely by his enemies for restraining himself from attacking them. See J. D. Mackie, *The Earlier Tudors*, Oxford, Clarendon Press, 1952, pp. 108–11. It is also significant that Henry's army, though it was paid off, was nevertheless dissatisfied with the arrangement, apparently at least in part, because the soldiers were disappointed in their expectation of booty. On war as an economic enterprise, and its relative unprofitability, see W. W. Rostow, *The Process of Economic Growth*, New York, Norton, 1952, Ch. 7, especially p. 155.

or grants given by a grateful king as a reward for military achievement constituted an important source of personal gain. True, such income expectations, like the supposed economic benefits of modern imperialist ventures, often proved ephemeral, but that is beside the point. Even though it was not always successful, it seems clear that medieval investment in the paraphernalia of war was undertaken partly for economic ends.

But while war enriched some individuals, and perhaps occasionally, some nations at the expense of others, it almost necessarily reduced over-all economic well-being. At best, as is sometimes said to have been true during the Wars of the Roses, although military activity used up productive resources in the manufacture of arms, the life of the people at large was not seriously affected. More frequently, economic welfare also was sharply reduced by direct destruction, as was surely the case in England under the Anarchy and in France during the worst periods of the Hundred Years' War or when The Conqueror or King John devastated large regions in response to rebellion.

Military investment, therefore, usually acts as a more powerful brake on productivity than does landholding. This may help to account for the relative lack of economic accomplishment in the Middle Ages, which was discussed by Marx and Engels.[19] But medieval war did not retard production primarily by its destructiveness. Modern wars are no doubt much better at that. More important, in my opinion, was a shortage of the means of recovery and further increases in output. The economy's meagre savings were largely dissipated in expenditures that may have been expected to yield private gain but were worse than unproductive. There was little economic incentive for individuals to behave otherwise.

5. Policy implications

I have been arguing that in some cases the rate of increase of productivity has been reduced, not primarily by expenditure on consumer durables, but by socially unproductive investment undertaken in the quest for wealth.

There is an important consequence for policy: if the wealthy saver is, in fact, uninterested in, or even repelled by, the thought of investing his wealth profitably, perhaps he can be induced to increase his contribution to the growth of national output only by a direct attack on his values. This is likely to be difficult to accomplish (or to justify). If, on the other hand, the investor is already looking for profits, it becomes a

[19]*Manifesto of the Communist Party*, Part I.

matter of convincing him that socially productive investments are also remunerative. The appropriate approach and strategy is different from that which can most effectively move the totally noneconomic spender. For example, sometimes the investor in socially unproductive assets may act as he does because institutional arrangements leave him little alternative. Weak enforcement of contracts or even hostile governmental behavior, as well as inexperience or lack of information, may well deter those who accumulate from turning to capitalistic enterprise. Some fairly obvious changes in government policy could in such circumstances markedly increase the inducement to invest productively.

Even if only *some* wealthier inhabitants of underdeveloped areas are economic men (which is really all that this chapter seeks to suggest), it may be good strategy to do everything possible to get these few to undertake socially productive investment. The argument is analogous with the Schumpeterian view that *"the appearance of one or a few entrepreneurs facilitates the appearance of others, and these the appearance of more, in ever-increasing numbers."*[20]

We shall return to these policy implications in Chapter 14.

6. Inducements to invest productively

Before closing the chapter, I shall discuss briefly what may have kept the modern capitalist economies from devoting as large a proportion of their savings to unproductive investment as do (or did) other economies. Like many other assets, unproductive investments can no doubt be expected, after some point, to yield diminishing returns to their owners. But their returns, by their very nature, may perhaps decline more rapidly and more sharply than the earnings of other assets. By definition, this type of investment adds nothing to national output. Whatever returns it yields to its owners must then be the result of a redivision of the pie, rather than of an increase in its size. But there are limits to the extent to which a fixed total can be redistributed. As the inequality of distribution grows more marked, resistance to still further increases in inequality will intensify. Resistance, of course, may take the obvious forms of revolt or protest growing out of the discontent of the impoverished. But more important for our purposes are the automatic counterforces produced by redistribution, which can frequently be counted upon to make further redivision of national product increasingly difficult. These may take the form of a combination of rigidities and flexibilities in the institutional arrangement.

[20]J. Schumpeter, *The Theory of Economic Development*, Cambridge, Mass., Harvard University Press, 1934, p. 228 (Schumpeter's italics).

For example, unproductive investment in land may yield diminishing returns because rents are relatively sticky, so that, though the inflation of land values in response to increased demand for land can continue to yield capital gains, the rent return per dollar of investment will decline. Moreover, as I noted in Section 3 of this chapter, the inflation in land values may sometimes lead to rising wages and increases in other prices (flexible prices and relatively inflexible living standards or demands for nonland inputs). This obviously can reduce the real value of the capital gains that result from rising land prices.

I conclude that, as the magnitude of an economy's investment grows, it will very likely become increasingly unprofitable to specialize in unproductive investment. More and more people will be forced to seek wealth in productive activity and, by the example of their success, they will make it easier and more tempting for others to follow.[21]

There is probably a more important institutional reason why productive capital constitutes a large proportion of the asset holdings of the modern firm. By and large, firms are organized primarily around some productive activity, and while some of their expenditure is directed to modifying the terms of sale and sometimes even to increasing consumers' misinformation, much of it is bound to go to their production and distribution processes. This is because, by the nature of its operations, increases and improvements in its stock of productive capital by the modern firm certainly will be among its convenient lucrative opportunities.

[21]However, it will always be possible for a few investors to do spectacularly well by the creation of assets that help them to redistribute incomes in their own favor while not adding to, or even while reducing, the total product. The destructive activity of Jay Gould is the most notorious example of this sort of success. But a few such spectacular cases can sometimes lead an army of hopefuls to try their hands at it even though, as in the gambling casino, the odds are clearly stacked against them.

CHAPTER 14

The critical role of expansion effort

From the point of view of development planning there is much wisdom in the simple proposition that (to paraphrase Professor Solow),[1] if a pair of twins leave different amounts in two banks, one offering 3 percent and one 3.01 percent, the twin using the latter bank will eventually hold the larger deposit.

Of course it must not be forgotten that, given enough of a head start, the lower interest twin may stay ahead for a very long time. Even if we are willing to concern ourselves with the very distant future we must be careful in accepting the applicability of the conclusion because we can have little confidence that the model will even vaguely approximate the facts for very long. One or both of the banks may fail, a twin may start living off his capital, interest rates can change, or a bomb may make the entire analysis irrelevant. "Eventually" can lie in the very distant future and it may never even come. Nevertheless, the basic point that the rate of compounding can eventually swamp most other influences must never be forgotten in formulating really long-run economic policy. The underdeveloped countries may find that at best they can hope to overtake the economically advanced countries only slowly and gradually. In such a plan the rate of compounding must be considered crucial.[2]

Moreover, I am convinced that the differences among the different economies to which the allegory of the twins refers are not so small that we must wait very long for them to show up. I shall come back to this

---

[1]See his review of Haavelmo's *A Study in the Theory of Economic Evolution* in the *American Economic Review*, Vol. XLV, March 1955, p. 155.

[2]The very great power of compounding is rather strikingly illustrated by the observation that a first folio Shakespeare, which is surmised to have sold for one pound when it was published in 1626, is today valued at about £10,000 for a copy in first-class condition. But had one pound instead been lent in 1623 at 5 percent, compounded annually, the principal would now have reached some 10 million pounds.

point after examining the policy implications of my construction in greater detail.

1. Policy suggested by the analysis

The implications of the compounding proposition are fairly obvious. A development program that concentrates on obtaining machinery from abroad will enable the importing nation to increase its rate of growth. But, unless this is accompanied by a more fundamental development program, the gain is likely to be transitory. Getting firms or foreign governments to build factories in underdeveloped areas also can be expected to yield disappointing results, even if the natural endowments of the areas are appropriate in terms of comparative advantage.[3] This is not meant to deny that foreign capital can be essential in the initial stages of a development program. But it does imply that unless capital imports constitute only one feature in a larger development plan they are likely to have little long-run effect on economic growth. In the long run, hope for these areas must rest on increases in productivity, in the rate of technological advance, and in internal saving and invest-ment, that is, on increases in what for expository purposes I will call their *index of expansion effort*.[4] In other words, the nation's resources must be more fully utilized in every productive process, and more of every unit of production must be devoted to increasing future pro-ductivity rather than to current consumption. Eventually these can add up, or multiply, to make a substantial difference in the nation's living levels.

[3] For a discussion in which heavy reliance is placed on the import of foreign capital, see R. Nurkse, *Problems of Capital Formation in Underdeveloped Countries*, 4th ed., Oxford, Blackwell, 1955, pp. 77–79. But Nurkse does state that "there is no solution to the problem without steady and strenuous effort on the domestic front. In a sense, therefore, it all boils down to this: capital is made at home," pp. 140–41.

[4] The view expressed is not uncommon; e.g., "It would probably be true to say that in every major case of really substantial, continuous development the great bulk of the capital has been supplied internally by the domestic processes of capital formation. Imports of capital, where present, have been mainly important as catalytic agents—often because they also brought technical knowledge . . . for development to 'take,' social institutions have to be built up and new social habits have to be formed which will achieve and maintain a higher level of internal capital formation. These institutions must handle two problems, because capital formation is a double-sided process: (1) The population must be induced or forced to consume less than the whole annual output, that is, to save—directly or indirectly; (2) The margin between total output and total consumption must be directed into productive investment which will increase the country's capacity to produce in subsequent years." E. Staley, *The Future of Underdeveloped Countries*, New York, Harper & Row, 1954, pp. 261–62.

More specifically, this points to criteria on which the developer's funds might be better allocated. An educational program that promises to increase the skills and the willingness of the population to work[5] may in the end pay off better than purchasing a batch of harvesters, no matter what their relative cost. Also, a revision in the tax laws conducive to productive investment should be given high priority. But here again, it must be recognized that particular types of capital imports, carefully chosen and carefully employed, can be justified on the grounds that they either increase the public's willingness to work or that they make a substantial contribution to the marginal productivity of labor. To sum up once more, the moral is not that capital imports should be minimized, but that they should be screened carefully and undertaken only as part of a promising over-all development program.

2. Increased expansion effort and fixed growth goals

The only moderately novel element in the preceding conclusion lies in the implication that there are no other means open to a slowly growing economy trying to speed up its rate of growth. It can never catch up by policy measures that fail to raise its index of expansion effort to the level characteristic of areas of rapid expansion and then keep it there.

This is not as strong a statement as it may seem. It does not assert that all other problems involved in economic development are, in comparison, unimportant (though I am inclined to believe that many of them are). So far I only have maintained that a rise in expansion effort is a *necessary* condition for relatively rapid growth. Doubtless there are other necessary conditions, some of which will vary from economy to economy. But the crucial property of *any* necessary condition for the achievement of an objective is that its violation absolutely precludes attainment of the objective.

The policy problem on which I have sought to focus attention may be on a par with other necessary conditions for growth. For example, a *persistently* high level of unemployment can deter growth in precisely the same way as does a low level of productivity per employed worker. I have already pointed out that fulfillment of the necessary condition I have chosen to emphasize, for a variety of reasons, may prove insufficient for the attainment of a specific growth objective.

[5]Professor Lewis (*The Theory of Economic Growth*, Homewood, Illinois, Irwin, 1955, p. 39) seems to argue that harder work which takes the form of longer hours can produce higher living standards but not more *rapidly growing* living standards. Apparently this is meant to apply only where there is no resulting increase in productive investment that can increase the rate of compounding.

3. Further importance of expansion effort

But it is my inclination to attach somewhat more significance to the need for a rise in the index of expansion effort than follows simply from its acceptance as a necessary condition. I have discussed growth targets and the necessary and sufficient conditions for their achievement as though some particular rate of growth (that of the most rapidly expanding economies) were peculiarly meritorious. In fact, other things being equal, the generally accepted position seems to be the more growth the merrier. With a target of such flexibility, partial solutions can also be desirable, for success in tackling any one of the relevant problems by itself may suffice to produce some significant acceleration in the per capita flow of goods. Viewed in this way, different policy measures may be considered to offer different potential contributions to growth, and it is my contention that, in the long run, the greatest of these payoffs may be expected from a rise in the index of expansion effort from a low level to one more nearly comparable with that in the rapidly growing economies.

I have argued that these payoffs, in the long run, certainly will be greater than those that ordinarily can be expected from haphazard gifts of capital to underdeveloped areas and other measures whose effects are analogous with an increase in the principal (the initial resource endowment of the economy) rather than with a rise in the interest rate, that is, in its rate of compounded growth.

Even among the measures that affect the rate of compounding directly, the potential returns of a significant rise in the index of expansion effort appear to be unusually great. Unwillingness to work hard, to invest productively, and resistance to innovation are peculiarly persistent problems. It is true that prolonged depressions and unemployment, as just indicated, can be expected to retard growth in the same way as does low productivity, but significant shortages of effective demand have usually been temporary and of short duration in comparison with the long periods relevant for economic growth.[6] There is little reason to believe that there have been parallel ups and downs in the expansion effort indices in underdeveloped areas. Unemployment is characteristically epidemic; low productivity[7] and the related difficulties are more frequently pandemic.

---

[6]It is a central contention of Ch. 12, above, that this is no historical accident. In the long run I believe that the pecuniary drives of the members of the economy will keep up investment demand sufficiently to restore more or less full employment.

[7]Under this heading we must properly include most cases of "disguised underemployment and unemployment" that have been cited in the literature. The relevant

4. The significance of relative incomes

There is yet another phenomenon that adds to the significance of the index of expansion effort. Professor Nurkse has reminded us that poverty and well-being are relative terms and that low levels of income are essentially measured in terms of the per capita income levels in the wealthiest countries.[8] After all, in absolute terms the standard of living of a moderately wealthy baron in the early Middle Ages in many ways would be unacceptable to a modern American slum dweller. The former was wealthy largely by comparison with his contemporaries.

This implies that an increase in per capita incomes in underdeveloped areas is not enough. The objectives of a development program must be more ambitious. To reduce poverty it is necessary to reduce *the gap* between per capita outputs in the richest and the poorest countries. But while programs designed to stimulate growth are undertaken in impoverished regions, the wealthier economies will not stay still and wait until they catch up. I have already discussed the tremendous pressures making for continued expansion in our own economy, and I see no reason to expect them to abate. It follows that, unless in backward areas the index of expansion effort (or rather, the complex of activity levels it represents) is raised to a level comparable with ours, the disparity between us will widen even further. To the extent that poverty is relative, the underdeveloped region must then be subject to the unhappy paradox of increasing poverty despite increasing output, not because of maldistribution within its own borders, but simply because that economy has not been able to run quickly enough to stand still.

5. Some recent examples

The hypothesis that there is a relatively high potential return to policy measures that can increase the index of expansion effort appears to be consistent with the evidence provided by some recent examples of

---

distinction from ordinary "Keynesian unemployment" is that the former does not usually refer to cases where productivity is low because of lack of effective demand. More frequently we must look to sociology or nutrition for the explanation of the low productivity levels which characterize disguised unemployment. The only source of ambiguity in the classification of disguised unemployment lies in the possibility that this sort of low productivity reduces effective demand, which in turn leads to further cuts in output per worker. This question of classification is no terminological quibble. Involved is the substantive problem of the appropriate policy measures. The use of Keynesian fiscal and monetary techniques in an attempt to reduce disguised unemployment whose source lies largely in institutionalized inability to work hard or efficiently may lead only to inflation. *Cf.* R. Nurkse, *op. cit.*, p. 36.

[8] R. Nurkse, *op. cit.*, pp. 58–65.

accelerated growth that will now be discussed. However, I must admit that these discussions are so superficial and impressionistic that they can bear little weight as evidence. In the final analysis, my choice of emphasis must be described as at least part conjecture or, at most, hypothesis.

The American case against which the growth of others is usually measured would appear to be at least superficially in line with our analysis. Productivity of labor seems to be very high, and the forces making for a high level of productive investment have already been discussed at length. But the case of the United States is not really very helpful because it involves many other favorable conditions. Population is growing but not rapidly enough to cause trouble, our natural resources are abundant, and what is most troublesome from the point of view of "testing" the analysis, the stock of capital has been relatively high for a long time. Thus, it is difficult to assess in this case the relative importance of the productivity and the high level of investment as against a high "initial" stock of capital.

There are, however, two other examples that appear to provide better illustrations. These are postwar West Germany and the Soviet Union. I suspect that the astonishing recovery of the former can be accounted for to a large extent in terms of the elements emphasized in my analysis. Certainly, after the war Germany's capital stock was seriously reduced, and what was left was heavily damaged. Probably, its capital stock was in poorer condition than that of some other western European countries. Yet the recovery of its productive system seems to have been one of the most spectacular in western Europe. I think an important role was played by the much publicized skill and efficiency of the German workman and by conditions that led to a tremendous propensity to invest in productive capital.

When viewed on this same superficial level, the disquieting growth in the military and industrial potential of the Soviet Union from its economically backward condition after the Revolution seems again to accord roughly with the analysis of this book. Here again the very high propensity to invest often has been cited as a crucial factor, though productivity seems to be rather unimpressive. What is noteworthy is the implication that the drive making for a high propensity to invest can be supplied by central direction as well as by the forces of the free market.[9] What seems to be needed is some sustained push that can be

---

[9]But even in the Soviet Union the motivation for expansion effort has not been supplied entirely by coercion. The Stakhanovite movement, in which high remuneration and prestige were offered to the very productive worker, certainly seems to have played an important part. Thus, M. Dobb (*Soviet Planning and Labour in Peace*

supplied in any of a variety of ways, but that push must be unrelenting. The problem of the developer would appear to be the invention of mechanisms whereby such a force can be set up without producing a cure with which he is less happy than with the disease.

Let us return finally to an issue raised earlier in the chapter: the length of time involved in the long run that is relevant to our analysis. The German and Russian experiences certainly suggest that it need not always be so long a period that at its end we will all be dead. Particularly, this appears to be the lesson of the German experience where recovery hardly even began until the monetary reform of 1948. If one could but supply strong forces that make for expansion, hard work, and abstinence from consumption in order to provide producer goods, an impressive economic expansion might not be long in coming.

---

and War, London, Routledge, 1942, pp. 82–86) states that "Soviet experience demonstrates the efficacy of wage increases disproportionate to increases in productivity." (Cited in W. Moore, *Industrialization and Labor*, Ithaca, Cornell University Press, 1951, p. 88.) Particularly, the high rate of reward and honorific status accorded to scientists and the members of other learned professions can help to account for the Russians' phenomenally rapid transition (as someone has put it) "from peasants to spacemen in one generation."

CHAPTER 15

Policy for growth

1. Education, coercion, and pecuniary inducement

The reader may or may not acquiesce in my hypothesis that the greatest potential source of growth lies in the level of expansion effort, but I expect he will agree that the problem is important and that it has proved peculiarly intractable.

The relevant policy measures that usually have been envisaged are slow processes of education and propaganda designed to change ways of thinking and patterns of behavior over the long run. Such an approach is by no means unimportant, but it is at best discouragingly slow. As we do not really know how to educate men to want to do the things that make for economic growth, there is the possibility that it may not work at all. Even in totalitarian countries, where the effort to mold men's minds has been unsparing, none of the dictators has had sufficient confidence in the effectiveness of his propaganda efforts to abandon completely his reliance on the instruments of terror whereby his subjects have been kept in line. How much confidence can we have then in smaller scale, more haphazard methods designed to change the desires and values of a populace?

Perhaps then we must resign ourselves to take motivations as given and search instead for substitute measures to provide the appropriate stimuli. Such measures are indeed possible. For example, I have already suggested that the dictators have succeeded in providing a substitute motivation mechanism by the direct or indirect use of coercion.

The natural question, then, is whether there is not some more palatable substitute available to the nations who wish, as it were, to move up along their expansion effort curve but are unwilling to employ totalitarian methods.

The training of the economist should lead him to look first where he so often finds pay dirt—at the price mechanism. The answer would appear to be to make it sufficiently lucrative for the individual to behave in a way that makes for high productivity or sufficiently costly to fail to do so.[1]

But what if the population is largely uninterested in economic rewards? I have already discussed this question in Chapter 13, where I supported my belief that at least in those areas where development programs are being considered seriously, economic motivations do play a considerable role. By taxation or subsidy schemes, or by offering wage incentives in an appropriate manner and in adequate amounts (with higher wages offered only for larger outputs), the people can be induced to change their ways. At least the wealthy residents of under-developed areas can usually be relied upon to want to maintain or increase their wealth. My position is that, from the point of view of economic growth, the difficulty is not that the rich are uninterested in riches but that they are often able to add to their net worth by means that do little to increase production. This again implies that the wealthy residents of underdeveloped areas can perhaps be induced to change their behavior in a way that makes for a higher index of expansion effort by making it sufficiently unprofitable to do otherwise.

2. Elements of a productivity compensation policy

The success of some privately run incentive compensation plans for employees in underdeveloped areas suggests that a similar scheme may be appropriate on a national scale—fiscal policy being an appropriate instrument for these purposes. As is well known, any tax system affects incentives and the allocation of resources, and so it must influence the economy's rate of development. It is therefore worth considering a major and thoroughgoing revision in the tax structure to see whether the fiscal system can be used to encourage growth more effectively.[2]

Any proposal as radical as that I will now describe must unavoidably raise questions about its palatability and practicality. No doubt, less disturbing versions of the suggested fiscal arrangement can be designed, and in any event its details are vague because there is little experience on which to base them. Yet I believe that some such device will have to be considered seriously by any community that is willing to pay the price for a material increase in its rate of growth and yet wishes to minimize the degree of coercion employed in achieving it.

[1] I have already noted in the previous chapter that even the Soviet Union has made fairly extensive use of this sort of price incentive.

[2] Some provisions in our current tax structure already encourage expansion. The relatively low capital gains tax, e.g., encourages retention and reinvestment of earnings rather than their payment as dividends to stockholders.

This proposal undertakes to provide a pecuniary reward to enterprises whose decisions accord with the community's growth objectives and to do so in a manner that limits as little as possible the individual's freedom to make economic decisions, while not interfering with the use of fiscal measures as an instrument of stabilization policy—as a tool to combat both inflation and unemployment.

The device designed to meet these requirements is a two-part tax-subsidy arrangement that distributes payments to business firms on the basis of the growth of their output but simultaneously imposes on them taxes whose amounts are unrelated to their rate of expansion. Thus, management would be able to reduce the company's net tax bill by increasing its rate of growth; that is, the firm's marginal expansion cost would be cut correspondingly.

Specifically, this could be accomplished by subjecting the firm to an increase in its profits tax and by offering it simultaneously a tax rebate (exemption) whose absolute amount would be based on the absolute increase in the company's value added (net output) as compared to earlier years.[3] Perhaps an average rate of growth for the past few years (some sort of moving average) might be employed to avoid giving undue weight to temporary output fluctuations. There then would be some rate of growth in value added that would leave the company's net tax position unchanged. If it grew more slowly than this the company's

[3]One of the basic characteristics to be expected of an incentive compensation plan is that it be designed to reward those, and only those, activities that promote the chosen goals. This requirement is not nearly as trivial as it may seem. It is sometimes violated by business enterprises in adopting schedules for bonus payments to sales staff that often remunerate salesmen in accord with their contribution to proximate rather than ultimate objectives of the firm; e.g., even firms whose goal seems to be profit maximization may end up rewarding contribution to sales rather than contribution to profits and thus motivate salesmen to spend their time promoting easy to sell but relatively unprofitable items in the firm's product line. In some cases where this is not the intention of the executives things are sometimes made worse by attempted countermeasures. Occasionally, for example, they lower the compensation for sales of easy-to-sell items, which may lead the sales representative to push items that are neither profitable nor readily salable! There is an analogous desideratum for the tax-growth incentive proposal—insofar as possible, it must be designed to promote growth and not something that, like investment or profits, cannot always be depended upon to promote expansion even though it is *closely associated with* growth in per capita output. Thus, it may not do just to encourage private investment; as already noted, profitable investment in socially unproductive assets can even retard economic growth. That is why value added is suggested as the basis for the tax incentive calculation. However, depending on the ultimate objective of the growth promotion program, some other basis may turn out to be preferable.

tax bill would be larger than it would be in the absence of the arrangement, while a firm that exceeded this breakeven rate of growth would be a net gainer in terms of taxes.

Like the Keynesian stabilization policies, this proposal is an instrument that influences the economy only globally. It provides no direct interference with the decisions of the individual producer. Just as a reduction in interest rate does not force anyone to undertake a particular investment decision—it merely makes it more profitable for firms to undertake investments of their choice—so this tax proposal forces no company to expand its output but encourages firms to grow in any way they prefer.

Specifically, for this reason the value added figure on which the rebate calculation would be based would have to be measured not physically but in money terms (measuring commodities not in current prices but in terms of their prices on some appropriate base date).[4] In this way management will retain full freedom to change its product line whenever this seems appropriate—it will receive full tax credit if its increased value added is obtained through the production of commodity y, though last year it had been turning out only commodity x. This also means that the firm that operates in a field in which demands are characteristically inelastic will not be at a serious disadvantage in terms of the growth tax incentives. While it may be unable to expand rapidly in its initial area of activity, it will be possible for it to catch up by diversifying its product line to include items whose sales can readily be increased.

The proposal avoids interference with the normal stabilization functions of fiscal policy through the independence of its tax and its exemption rates. By setting its tax rates high and its scale of exemptions low the arrangement may be used to increase the government's net tax collections, while if the tax schedule is low and its exemption rates are generous it can serve to contribute to a deficit. The government, in effect, is given two degrees of freedom (the tax rate and the rebate rate) that enable it simultaneously to provide a fiscal growth incentive of whatever strength it desires (the level of growth-based rebates) while permitting it any fiscal surplus or deficit that its stabilization program calls for.

---

[4]The advantages for tax calculations of using a *pecuniary* measure rather than some physical index of growth in value added should be obvious enough. However, the use of an initial price level in the calculation seems unavoidable because otherwise entrepreneurs would be able to obtain larger tax exemptions simply by raising their prices more rapidly. The choice of base price and its occasional revision to take account of changing demand patterns is likely to prove a very troublesome business.

This, in outline, is my illustrative growth stimulation device. Because it is so radical it will undoubtedly seem impractical—perhaps more impractical than it is in fact—and because it increases the rewards of those who succeed and adds to the penalties of those who fail it is not likely to appeal to us on grounds of fairness. Yet that is just how the profit system always directs production and rewards efficiency. If we wish to encourage growth without abandoning the profit system and its implied freedom of economic choice there seems to be little alternative, except for the details of the arrangement.

I am not necessarily advocating the proposal that has just been described. Rather, I am arguing that increased growth requires us either to impose direct controls or to offer appropriate financial incentives. If an economy chooses as a goal a substantial increase in its growth rate, it must be prepared to undertake a program sufficiently drastic to achieve it. A program such as the one that has been described or some equally drastic substitute is the price of very rapid growth, and as in any other economic decision, rationality requires that the price be known and considered fully before a commitment actually is undertaken.

3. Some further comments on the growth proposal

This section expands somewhat on the discussion of the growth stimulation proposal, commenting in fairly unsystematic fashion on some of its features.

1. Instead of employing a set of taxes, it might be possible to achieve the same effect by means of a system of subsidies that are awarded instead of tax exemptions to those producers who expand their sales most rapidly. In some cases, because it is difficult to impose new taxes of an appropriate variety, it may be necessary to offer at least some subsidies of this sort in order to render the scheme at all practicable.

2. From the point of view of equity it may appear that the ideal arrangement is one in which a producer's exemption just covers the tax imposed upon him by the scheme if his rate of growth is just equal to some target level set by the government. In other words, if an over-all growth rate of 5 percent per year is considered reasonable, firms whose output grows more slowly than this should be penalized, while those that expand more rapidly would be rewarded.

However, several considerations argue against such a norm. First of all, its apparent equitability rests on a tacit assumption that the initial distribution of wealth is also equitable, for it roughly preserves the status quo distribution among all producers whose output grows by the same proportion. Second, it takes no account of the over-all fiscal objectives of the government. For example, in an inflationary situation it may be desirable to achieve a budget surplus, and it would appear reasonable to adjust tax and exemption levels accordingly. Of course, if surpluses and deficits were already determined in accord with these requirements before the adoption of the scheme, then policy-makers may well wish to determine the levels of the additional taxes and exemptions required by this proposal on the basis of an equity criterion related to that just described.

3. It may be desired to exempt some specified types of output partly, or wholly, from the scheme for political or even for economic reasons, for it may be decided that the output of some commodities should not be penalized by the taxes and that others should not benefit from exemptions or subsidies. For example, the developer may not wish to encourage growth in the production of luxury consumption goods that are not imported. However, if such goods are imported, their domestic production can save scarce foreign exchange, so that whether their output at home should be encouraged is a matter of political strategy or comparative advantage. In general, the list of exempted or partially exempted commodities should be kept very small.

State enterprises should also be included in such a program. The administrative details must vary from case to case, but two possibilities may be noted. If the nationalized industry is operated on a profit basis—that is, managers are told that they must earn a profit—state-owned enterprises can enter the scheme on the same terms as do private business firms. Where the operation is not conducted on a profit standard, it may be desirable to base the managers' salaries on the rate of growth of the firm—that is, to put them on an incentive compensation plan.

4. It should be made clear that the proposed tax arrangement offers no special advantage to the larger firm because the absolute payment is based on the absolute rate of growth. It would offer proportionately greater rewards to the small, rapidly growing business than it would to the static industrial giant. Indeed, in a line of business where there are marked diseconomies of scale, the large firm might, as seems appropriate from the point of view of national productive efficiency, be at a substantial disadvantage.

But the scheme as it stands, like any incentive to growth *per se*, can work for increased industrial concentration. If rewards are made for increased output and sales, it is equally profitable to achieve this either by adding to the output of the industry or at the expense of a competitor. Though the problem can certainly be serious, it is debatable how much, if anything, should be done about this in the fiscal arrangements. The tax exemption could be based partly on the rate of growth of the industry, but this leads to all sorts of administrative difficulties and can materially reduce the effectiveness of the plan. If monopolistic problems become too serious, an antitrust program, somewhat on the American line, will probably be more satisfactory.

5. Ideally, it would be hoped that the effects of the arrangement would trickle down in the economy. Producers who are forced to work for ever higher outputs would, it is hoped, be led to invest and innovate appropriately wherever they can. In addition, they might be induced to adopt policies that make for higher employee productivity. But, at least at first, it may be desirable to accelerate the process by offering special exemptions to firms that adopt piece wages or, better yet, wage plans that parallel the proposed tax arrangement.

4. Some of the problems

The details of any practical version of such a scheme (fortunately for the author) will have to be worked out case by case. The difficulties that beset such a proposal are sufficiently obvious. I will list only a few of the most obvious of these, largely without comment.

The political problems involved in getting the public to acquiesce to the adoption of such a scheme may be overwhelming. Because it is a plan designed to get people to do what they are not doing voluntarily, the arrangement is bound to be unpopular with some. It may be conjectured that resistance may be greatest in a country (like Britain) where a history of unemployment has led the public to regard high productivity with suspicion or outright hostility.

The difficulties of this political problem can perhaps be reduced if the program's promise to achieve the economic growth that is apparently desired is made clear to the public. But in some cases there nevertheless may be no alternative to the use of force to support government policies. However, there are different degrees in the use of coercive measures. Our government uses force to see that taxes are collected, but not to retain itself in office after it has been defeated at the polls.

Even in some highly developed countries the governments have never succeeded in working out an effective tax structure.[5] Some countries rely largely on import duties for their revenues. In such cases, subsidies

[5]One of the difficulties in underdeveloped areas has been the unwillingness of taxpayers to do the requisite bookkeeping. But where books must be kept in order to become eligible for tax exemptions or subsidies, one may be somewhat more sanguine about the prospects for cooperation, because it is then more directly in the entrepreneur's interest to keep these records.

rather than tax exemptions[6] may have to play the more important role. But the inflationary implications of such a decision can be serious and cannot be ignored by the planner.

There is danger that such a plan will lead to a very great extension of the administrative costs of government and in bureaucracy. Particularly the selection of individual commodity prices to be used in evaluation of growth in value added, and the adjudication of the consequent complaints is likely to require elaborate machinery. This may be considered wasteful as well as undesirable in and of itself because of the implied dangers to personal freedom. Unfortunately, this danger is implicit in almost any promising governmental program and, in that respect, the proposed program appears to be at least clearly preferable to a totalitarian alternative. At any rate, I believe that the problems of administration and bureaucracy can be minimized by keeping the program as automatic and undiscretionary in its operation as is possible.

Such a program can easily be frustrated by failure to take other appropriate and complementary policy measures. Illiteracy and lack of technical training, failure to provide roads, failure to restrain inflation, and shortages of effective demand leading to chronic unemployment can cripple a growth incentive policy.

In some cases the growth goals of an economy may be unattainable because of circumstances largely beyond the control of presently employed or presently known policy measures. Very rapid population growth or extreme poverty in natural resources may prevent any considerable rise in per capita real income.

This list of problems is nowhere near complete. I will make no attempt to minimize the difficulties specified and unspecified. I will only say that I do not believe them to be insurmountable. Unfortunately, because the methods for coping with them must vary so much from case to case, and because of the inadequacy of my own qualifications, I can say no more here than this. Once more, let it be clear that I am not advocating the adoption of growth as an appropriate objective. That is no decision to be taken lightly by any nation. But if this decision is taken, and taken seriously, the policy-makers must be willing to pay the required price. Profound results can usually be expected to require radical measures.

[6]It has been suggested to me that a high interest rate on overpaid taxes sometimes leads firms to be anxious to prepay their taxes. Possibly, then, such an interest rate and a prepayment-rebate provision may make compliance with the proposed tax scheme more attractive, unless the rate of inflation is so great that it eats up any feasible interest payments—a very real problem in some of the underdeveloped areas. In fact, inflation may make it desirable to have a simultaneous tax and exemption settlement, with the taxpayer submitting to the government only any excess of his tax over his exemption.

5. Epilogue

The unifying theme of Part II of this book is its preoccupation with the strategy rather than the tactics of growth. In this, I think it differs sharply from many studies of the problems of development and particularly from those concerned primarily with policy rather than theory. Studies of the problems of balance of payments, of banking practices, and other similar investigations relating to the underdeveloped areas, are of very great importance. Without a setting appropriate in its many details, the problems of the developer may be insuperable. But these tactical details do not get at the heart of the problem, for they fail to provide for the motor power to speed up the vehicle.

At the beginning of Part II, I cited Haavelmo's call for us to examine "the really big dissimilarities in economic life." I think this viewpoint is relevant here. I do not seek to detract from the very valuable contributions being made by the specialists, but if we examine the underdeveloped areas that are receiving substantial technical advice and financial assistance in their development programs, and compare their rate of economic progress with that of the Soviet economy that was itself so recently underdeveloped, it must be admitted that the rate of growth of the former is relatively unspectacular. Here, surely, is a big difference of the sort to which Haavelmo refers, and I have sought to provide an explanation and some appropriate policy measures.

The latter part of the volume has sought to examine some characteristics of the areas of more rapid growth and those of the areas of slower growth that I believe to be crucial in an explanation of the growth process. I have maintained that in all cases where growth has been rapid, it has been spurred on by arrangements that motivate the members of the economy to work hard for economic expansion. I have followed Schumpeter in his belief that in the Western economies these growth forces are to be found in the structure of our firms, and I suggest several ways in which this occurs in addition to that brought to our attention by Schumpeter.

I have maintained that elements of the same mechanism are to be found in many of the underdeveloped areas—the wealthy (and others) want to increase, or at least to maintain their wealth, whether for its own sake or because it permits them to pursue other objectives. What is lacking is an effective arrangement for translating this drive to acquire wealth into a force that promotes economic expansion.

The underdeveloped areas that wish to expand have open to them three ways to provide such an arrangement: the first alternative consists of slow and undependable steps designed to introduce Western capitalist institutions and attitudes that, without further governmental intervention, will get the people to behave in a manner that is conducive to growth. Their other two alternatives are the carrot and the stick. In totalitarian lands the efficacy of the stick has already been demonstrated. In this last chapter I have sought to outline the design of a carrot—a reward in the form of tax remittances to those who promote economic growth. It may not be the only possible carrot, but it is perhaps a prototype. At any rate, the prospects posed by the other alternatives—the regimented economy or the undependable and discouragingly slow battle to change the social structure—are bleak. A method that works by providing obvious rewards for appropriate efforts has the virtue that it holds out at least a faint hope to the impoverished.

Index

implications for, of Western capitalist growth mechanism, 120–21
ineffective tax structure in, 145
investment hypothesis for, 117
and rate of compounding proposition, 132–34
and significance of relative incomes, 136
unproductive use of savings as problem for. *See* Savings
wealthy increasing or maintaining wealth in, 140, 147
without socially productive investment, 130
Unemployment, 135, 145, 146
and disguised underemployment, 135*n*.–36*n*.
effective remedy for, 108
Utopian socialist schemes, 6

Veblen, T., 114*n*.
Viner, J., 84*n*., 125*n*.

Wage plans, 145
Walter, Hubert, 127*n*.
West Germany, postwar recovery of productive system in, 137–38
Western economy: and Soviet economy, policy proposal for, 85
Williamson, O. E., 51*n*., 67*n*.

Young, A. A., 22
Young Presidents Organization, 47